First-year Composition Guide

2010 Edition

Our Green initiatives include:

Electronic Products
We deliver products in non-paper form whenever possible. This includes pdf downloadables, flash drives, & CDs.

Electronic Samples
We use Xample, a new electronic sampling system. Instructor samples are sent via a personalized web page that links to pdf downloads.

FSC Certified Printers
All of our printers are certified by the Forest Service Council which promotes environmentally and socially responsible management of the world's forests. This program allows consumer groups, individual consumers, and businesses to work together hand-in-hand to promote responsible use of the world's forests as a renewable and sustainable resource.

Recycled Paper
Most of our products are printed on a minimum of 30% post-consumer waste recycled paper.

Support of Green Causes
When we do print, we donate a portion of our revenue to green causes. Listed below are a few of the organizations that have received donations from Fountainhead Press. We welcome your feedback and suggestions for contributions, as we are always searching for worthy initiatives.

Rainforest 2 Reef
Environmental Working Group

Book design by Susan Moore
Cover Design by Doris Bruey

For information, please call or write:

1-800-586-0330
Fountainhead Press
Southlake, TX. 76092

Web site: www.fountainheadpress.com
Email: customerservice@fountainheadpress.com

Third Edition

ISBN: 978-1-59871-398-5

Printed in the United States of America

Table of Contents

Chapter One Introduction to First-year Composition 1

Administration 3

Why Write? FYC and Academic Discourse 3

Chapter Two Description of First-year Composition Courses 5

English 1101: First-year Composition I 7

English 1102: First-year Composition II 8

English 1102m: Multicultural First-year Composition II 10

Honors Courses for First-year Composition 11

English Composition for ESOL Students 12

First-year Composition Online 12

Alternative Approaches to First-year Composition: 12

- Special Topics
- UGA Learning Communities
- FYC in Franklin Residential College
- Reacting to the Past

Chapter Three Policies and Procedures 15

Placement 17

Absences 18

Grade Appeals 18

Incompletes 19

General Grading Weights 19

Plus/Minus Grading 20

Chapter Four Using <emma>™ in the First-year Composition Program 21

Brief Introduction to <emma>™ 23

<emma>™ Lab and Support Team (Frogs) 36

Chapter Five Evaluation of Essays in the First-year Composition Program 39

What Do Teachers Want? 41

What Grades on Essays Mean 42

The Grading Rubric 43

Using the Rubric's Vocabulary 44

Chapter Six Electronic Portfolios in the First-year Composition Program 55

Elements of the Portfolio 57

How Are FYC Portfolios Evaluated? 61

Chapter Seven Academic Honesty and Plagiarism 65
Introduction: Academic Honesty and Plagiarism 67
Workshop: How Not to Plagiarize 68
Handout: "Citation or Plagiarism? Using Sources Wisely" 70
Chapter Eight Resources 71
Tutoring 73
UGA Libraries 74
CAPS 75
Chapter Nine What Comes Next? 77
Writing Certificate Program 79
Writing Intensive Program (WIP) 80
The Major and Minor in English 80
Bulldog Book Club 81
Advanced Courses in Writing 81
Chapter Ten Barnett Essay Awards for 2009-2010 83
English 1101: Macy Marie Sirmans, "A Profile of Pirate Football" 85
English 1101: John Mays, "'Maharaj Cotton': How the Death of 'King Cotton' Led to Increased British Interests in India" 96
English 1101: Olivia Swint, "Rise Against: Speaking Out Against War" 102
English 1102: Darcy Lenz, "Father Knows Best" 108
English 1102m: Mariana Heredia, "Crime and Punishment – Egyptian Style" 114
Chapter Eleven Michael G. Moran Electronic Portfolio Awards for 2009-2010 119
English 1101: Trevor Spears 121
English 1102: Katie Ali Farhani 130
English 1102m: Teneil Anesia Salmon 139
Chapter Twelve Appendix 163
Robert Leamnson, "Learning (Your First Job)" 165
Terms for English 1101, 1102, and 1102m 177

CHAPTER ONE

Introduction to First-year Composition

1

First-year Composition Program

Office: 128 Park Hall
Telephone: (706) 542-2128

Staff:
Dr. Christy Desmet, Director
Dr. Deborah Church Miller, Associate Director
Dr. Erin Presley, Assistant Director
Ms. Jane Barroso, Administrative Assistant II
jbarroso@uga.edu

Why Write? FYC and Academic Discourse

Writing is more than simply recording our thoughts, observations, and conclusions. Often it is a way of discovering what we think or feel. If it were merely the transcribing of what is in our minds, writing would never cause us any problems. Yet how many times have you sat down to write, thinking you knew what you wanted to express, only to find that your thoughts were jumbled or half-formed? Or you may have begun a writing assignment with nothing to say, but found, as you wrote, that you had a range of opinions and information about your subject. In both cases, you discovered what you actually knew or thought only in the act of writing.

Scholars and researchers have long known that writing is itself "a way of knowing." The act of writing improves comprehension of academic material and fixes that material in our memories. This benefit of using writing to master and recall information is discussed further in Robert Leamnson's brief essay, "Learning (Your First Job)," which is included in this book. Even more important, writing can play an important role in the process of learning itself. Writing helps us to make connections among different pieces of information and between information and ideas; it also provides us with a visible record of those connections and (for instance, in the case of multiple drafts) shows us how our ideas change over time. In Leamnson's terms, writing allows us to produce not just "information," but "knowledge."

The kind of writing focused on in FYC is called academic discourse. At the University of Georgia, you will be asked to do many different kinds of writing for your classes. As you move into your academic major toward graduation, you will become increasingly involved in writing tasks that draw on specific genres and conventions for your academic field. Psychologists, for instance, engage in different kinds of research and writing than do literary critics. First-year Composition cannot prepare you directly for all these advanced experiences in writing; what we do instead is to give you a grounding in academic discourse, which lays a foundation for later thinking and writing experiences by practicing kinds of writing that seek to inform and persuade a range of audiences. In FYC courses, you will do research on various topics (seek out information) and, together with your teacher and fellow students, work through writing and discussion to use that information to produce knowledge. You will also test the persuasiveness of your knowledge for a variety of audiences, including your teacher, peers, and others.

Two other important goals of FYC are the arts of revision and collaboration. For each writing assignment, FYC classes engage in drafting and revision, and for each they engage as well in peer review. You get the opportunity to demonstrate your proficiency in these two crucial areas in the Composing/Revision and Peer Review exhibits in the Electronic Portfolio that you submit as your final requirement in the course. (The Electronic Portfolio is discussed in detail later in this book.) Your skill in these areas will stand you in good stead as you leave your current teacher and classmates, moving through the core curriculum and your major at the University of Georgia. Finally, our program emphasizes writing in the new electronic environments that are important not only to academics and the world of business, but also to individuals in their private lives. You will use a variety of technologies in your work for FYC, in particular the program's own electronic writing environment <emma>™ for your work during the semester and for constructing your final Electronic Portfolio for the course.

The Instructors and Administration of UGA's First-year Composition Program sincerely hope that you enjoy your experiences with writing this year and that you leave our program with the skills and work habits necessary to succeed in writing tasks throughout the curriculum. More broadly, we hope that you leave us feeling confident of your critical thinking, your composing and revision skills, and your ability to comment intelligently on your own and others' writing. Finally, we hope that you will continue to enjoy and practice writing during your years at the university. For that reason, we will give you information later about further opportunities for reading and writing at UGA.

CHAPTER TWO

Description of First-year Composition Courses

2

All FYC courses share a set of core goals, or learning outcomes, which are detailed below and are also reflected in the program grading rubric and electronic portfolio assignment (both of which are discussed in greater detail later in this Guide).

English 1101: First-year Composition I

English 1101 focuses on informational, analytical, and argumentative writing (the principal genres of academic discourse that students will encounter in many courses across the curriculum), and on research skills and critical thinking. While there are different varieties of English 1101 classes and instructors design their own syllabi, you can get a general sense of what an English 1101 course looks like by consulting the ENGL 1101 Sample Syllabi posted on the First-year Composition Program's website, available online through the English Department Home Page at: http://www.english.uga.edu/.

Prerequisites:

Students must either place into English 1101 or pass out of the Academic Enhancement Program.

Goals:

In English 1101 students will learn to:

⇒ write papers in and out of class using processes that include discovering ideas and evidence, organizing that material, and revising, editing, and polishing the finished paper;

⇒ think critically so that they can recognize the difference between opinion and evidence and so that they can support an intelligent, challenging thesis;

⇒ address papers to a range of audiences;

⇒ understand the collaborative and social aspects of the writing process and demonstrate an ability to critique the writing of themselves and others;

⇒ develop a sense of voice appropriate to the subject, the writer's purpose, the context, and the reader's expectations;

⇒ understand how genres shape reading and writing and produce writing in several genres;

⇒ follow the conventions of standard edited English and MLA documentation;

⇒ use electronic environments for drafting, reviewing, revising, editing, and sharing texts;

⇒ understand and exploit the differences in the rhetorical strategies and in the affordances available for both print and electronic composing processes and texts.

Requirements:

Students will write a minimum of three essays (1,000-1,500 words or longer) that count for at least 50% of the student's final grade. In addition to writing papers and doing other work, all students will create a final electronic portfolio that counts approximately as one-third of their final grade. The ePortfolio is discussed at greater length below.

Course Texts:

Lunsford, ed. *The St. Martin's Handbook*, 6th ed.
Rosenwasser and Stephen, *Writing Analytically*, 5th ed.
First-year Composition Guide, 2010 ed. (Fountainhead Press)
Any standard college dictionary, such as:

American Heritage Dictionary
Random House College Dictionary
Webster's New Collegiate Dictionary
Webster's New World Dictionary

English 1102: First-year Composition II

Prerequisites:

To enroll in English 1102, students must have either exempted English 1101 or passed it with a "D" or better. To graduate, however, students must have earned a grade of "C" in English 1101 and have a combined average grade of "C" in English 1101 and 1102/1102m. Students therefore are strongly advised not to enroll in English 1102/1102m until they have received a "C" in English 1101.

According to the University policy on plus-minus grading, a grade of "C-" will not satisfy the requirement for a "C" in ENGL 1101; a combined average of "C-" or 1.7 in English 1101 and 1102 will not satisfy the requirement for a combined average of "C" in the two courses. For more information on plus-minus grading, see:

http://www.bulletin.uga.edu/PlusMinusGradingFAQ.html

FAQ #9 is particularly relevant to the requirements of First-year Composition.

Goals:

English 1102 shares the core goals, or learning outcomes, of English 1101, but includes as well other goals specific to the course. The content also varies: while English 1101 focuses on different varieties of non-fiction writing, English 1102 focuses on informational, analytical, and argumentative writing through literary texts in various genres; as in English 1101 and English 1102m, research and critical thinking skills are also emphasized. While there are different varieties of English 1102 classes, and instructors design their own syllabi, you can get a general sense of what an English 1102 course looks like by consulting the ENGL 1102 Sample Syllabi posted on the First-year Composition Program's website, available online through the English Department Home Page at: http://www.english.uga.edu/.

In English 1102 students will learn to:

- ⇒ read, appreciate, and interpret fiction, drama, and poetry and write analytically about them;
- ⇒ understand literary principles and use basic terms important to critical writing and reading;
- ⇒ write papers in and out of class using processes that include discovering ideas and evidence, organizing that material, and revising, editing, and polishing the finished paper;
- ⇒ think critically so that they can recognize the difference between opinion and evidence and so that they can support an intelligent, challenging thesis, and more specifically, document essays using textual evidence;
- ⇒ address papers to a range of audiences;
- ⇒ understand the collaborative and social aspects of the writing process and demonstrate an ability to critique the writing of themselves and others;
- ⇒ develop a sense of voice appropriate to the subject, the writer's purpose, the context, and the reader's expectations;
- ⇒ understand how genres shape reading and writing and produce writing in several genres;
- ⇒ follow the conventions of standard edited English and MLA documentation;
- ⇒ use electronic environments for drafting, reviewing, revising, editing, and sharing texts;
- ⇒ understand and exploit the differences in the rhetorical strategies and in the affordances available for both print and electronic composing processes and texts.

Requirements:

Students will write a minimum of three essays (1,000-1,500 words or longer) that count for at least 50% of the student's final grade. In addition to writing papers and doing other work, all students will create a final electronic portfolio that counts approximately as one-third of their final grade. The ePortfolio is discussed at greater length below.

Course Texts:

Lunsford, ed. *The St. Martin's Handbook*, 6th ed.
Clifford and Schilb, eds. *Making Literature Matter*, 4th ed., or Desmet, Hart, and Miller, eds., *Prentice Hall Literature Portfolio*, or another approved text of the instructor's choice
First-year Composition Guide, 2010 ed. (Fountainhead Press)
Any standard college dictionary, such as:
American Heritage Dictionary
Random House College Dictionary
Webster's New Collegiate Dictionary
Webster's New World Dictionary

English 1102m: Multicultural First-year Composition II

Description:

English 1102m focuses on developing effective critical writing, reading, and research skills, using core texts that explore the multicultural dimensions of American literature and culture, with an emphasis on African American, Latino/a American, Asian-American, and/or Native American literary traditions. This course offers three hours of credit toward the First-year Composition requirement as well as the Franklin College Multicultural Literacy requirement. While English 1102m instructors design their own syllabi, you can get a general sense of what an English 1102m course looks like by consulting the ENGL 1102m Sample Syllabi posted on the First-year Composition Program's website, available online through the English Department Home Page at: http://www.english.uga.edu/.

Goals:

In English 1102m students will learn to:

⇒ read, appreciate, and interpret fiction, drama, and poetry — with an emphasis on African American, Latino/a American, Asian-American, and/or Native American literary traditions — and write analytically about them;

⇒ situate literature in the historical and cultural context of production and reception;

⇒ understand literary principles and use basic terms important to critical writing and reading;

⇒ write papers in and out of class using processes that include discovering ideas and evidence, organizing that material, and revising, editing, and polishing the finished paper;

⇒ think critically so that they can recognize the difference between opinion and evidence and so that they can support an intelligent, challenging thesis, and more specifically, document essays using textual evidence;

⇒ address papers to a range of audiences;

⇒ understand the collaborative and social aspects of the writing process and demonstrate an ability to critique the writing of themselves and others;

⇒ develop a sense of voice appropriate to the subject, the writer's purpose, the context, and the reader's expectations;

⇒ understand how genres shape reading and writing and produce writing in several genres;

⇒ follow the conventions of standard edited English and MLA documentation;

⇒ use electronic environments for drafting, reviewing, revising, editing, and sharing texts;

⇒ understand and exploit the differences in the rhetorical strategies and in the affordances available for both print and electronic composing processes and texts.

Requirements:

Students will write a minimum of three essays (1,000-1,500 words or longer) that count for at least 50% of the student's final grade. In addition to writing papers and doing other work, all students will create a final electronic portfolio that counts approximately as one-third of their final grade. The ePortfolio is discussed at greater length below.

Course Texts:

Lunsford, ed. *The St. Martin's Handbook*, 6th ed.
Schmidt, Crockett, and Bogarad, eds., *Portable Legacies, Custom Edition* or an other approved text of the instructor's choice
First-year Composition Guide, 2010 ed. (Fountainhead Press)
Any standard college dictionary, such as:
- *American Heritage Dictionary*
- *Random House College Dictionary*
- *Webster's New Collegiate Dictionary*
- *Webster's New World Dictionary*

Honors Courses for First-year Composition II

Description:

Honors students have the option of substituting for English 1102 either English 1050H (Composition and Literature) or English 1060H (Composition and Multicultural Literature). These courses have the same general goals as other First-year Composition courses at the University of Georgia, but each class is designed individually by the instructor, often around a special topic.

English Composition for ESOL Students

Description:

Special sections of English 1101 and 1102/1102m are reserved for students who have a native language other than American English and who can benefit from an English for Speakers of Other Languages (ESOL) emphasis in these classes. Students enroll only with the permission of the department (POD), but the classes are not marked differently on their transcripts. The ESOL sections, like the classes for native speakers, focus on writing academic argument in English 1101 and writing about literature in English 1102/1102m. In addition to offering three hours of credit toward the First-year Composition requirement, English 1102m will also fulfill a graduation requirement of the College of Arts and Sciences for a course in multicultural studies.

First-year Composition classes for ESOL offer non-native speakers opportunities for vocabulary development, for grammar practice, and for orientation to American styles of writing and organization. Residents of the United States whose first language is not American English, as well as international students, may qualify for these classes. To determine your eligibility and to obtain a POD to register for the ESOL classes, contact the First-year Composition Program Office (706-542-2128).

First-year Composition Online

Description:

Each semester, the Program offers several English 1101 and 1102/1102m sections taught via the Internet and the World Wide Web. First-year Composition Online has the same goals and requirements as other FYC classes at the University of Georgia: our version of the course has an additional advantage in that it asks students to communicate through writing frequently and in different contexts.

Alternative Approaches to First-year Composition

The First-year Composition Program is involved in a number of innovative programs on campus and offers several alternative versions of its core courses. Each of these courses has the same prerequisites, goals, and requirements as the more traditional versions.

⇒ **Special Topics:** Experienced instructors may design a special topics version of FYC that is approved in advance by the First-year Composition Committee. These courses often focus on topics related to the instructor's research or scholarly interests, and the sections are marked by a special note in OASIS.

⇒ **UGA Learning Communities:** The FYC Program has played a major role in the development of UGA's Learning Communities. As part of each Learning Community, students take a First-year Composition class that is linked to the theme of the LC and sometimes to the content of their other courses in the LC. A description of the UGA Learning Communities and a current list of LC's being offered may be found online at: http://www.uga.edu/learningcommunities/.

⇒ **FYC in the Franklin Residential College:** Each Fall semester the FYC Program offers one section of First-year Composition for the Franklin Residential Community. This special class is designed specifically for the community by the instructor. For more information on the FRC, see http://www.uga.edu/frc/.

⇒ **Reacting to the Past:** The FYC Program has now begun to offer sections of composition that incorporate the innovative pedagogy of UGA's Reacting to the Past curriculum. You can find out more about Reacting at the University of Georgia at: http://www.reacting.uga.edu/.

CHAPTER THREE

Policies and Procedures

3

Placement

Most university students will take English 1101 and 1102/1102m during their first year at UGA. However, some students will receive credit for these courses based on the following tests:

1. The Advanced Placement Test. Students who earn a score of 3 or 4 on the National Advanced Placement Test in Literature or Composition receive three hours of credit for English 1101; those who earn a score of 5 receive six hours of credit for English 1101 and 1102. All AP equivalencies are available on the Registrar's website:
   http://www.reg.uga.edu/or.nsf/html/uga_ap_credit_equivalencies
2. The International Baccalaureate (IB) Test. Students who earn a score of 4, 5, or 6 on the International Baccalaureate Test at the Higher Level (HL) in English receive three hours of credit for English 1101; those who earn a score of 7 on the International Baccalaureate Test at the Higher Level (HL) receive six hours of credit for English 1101 and 1102. **For diploma recipients only,** students who earn a score of 5, 6, or 7 on the Standard Level (SL) test receive three hours of credit for English 1101.
3. The Departmental Placement Test. Beginning in Fall 2003, students not placed by a national placement test will fall into two groups. Students with an SATV score of 590 and above or an ACT score of 26 or above will place automatically in ENGL 1101 and may register for that class without any further testing; if these students choose to do so, they may take the Departmental Placement Test voluntarily with an eye to exempting English 1101 with three hours of credit. Students with an SATV score of 580 or below are **required** to take the Departmental Placement Test before registering for a First-year Composition class. Specific information about the Departmental English Placement Test can be found at the Testing Services Website: http://www.testing.uga.edu/english.php

The Departmental English Placement Test consists of two parts, mechanics and rhetoric. A score of 22 (part 1) and 20 (part 2) will place students in English 1102 and give them three hours of credit for English 1101. Students whose test scores indicate that they might have trouble in English 1101 will write an essay to determine whether they will be advised to take English 1101 or an Academic Enhancement class.

Students should take the test at a First-year Orientation Session. Those who miss the test at Orientation may take it later at University Testing Services in Clark Howell Hall. However, the test is not open to students who have taken or are currently enrolled in First-year Composition here or elsewhere. For more information, please call (706) 542-3183 or visit the website: http://www.uga.edu/testing/.

Absences

Because writing skills develop slowly over time and because in-class activities are crucial to the final Portfolio, students' regular attendance is essential in First-year Composition. Consequently, on the fifth absence (MWF classes) or the fourth absence (TTh classes), no matter what the reason, students can expect to be dropped either with a WP or a WF before the midpoint of the semester and with a WF after midpoint. For summer session, on the fourth absence, no matter what the reason, students can expect to be dropped either with a WP or a WF before the midpoint of the semester and with a WF after midpoint.

Grade Appeals

It is the instructor's responsibility to judge work and assign grades. Consequently, students with questions about final grades should first discuss those questions with their instructors. If the problem cannot be resolved in discussion, students may prepare a grade appeal in writing according to the new guidelines established by the Franklin College Bylaws, Article V. The bylaws are available at:

http://www.franklin.uga.edu/fac_staff/govern/bylaws.htm

In First-year Composition appeals, the Director of First-year Composition replaces the Department Head of English in the appeals procedure, in accordance with the English Department bylaws. Once a ruling on the grade appeal has been made, if either the student or instructor wants to take the appeal further, the appeal will be conducted according to the guidelines set out in Section III, "Appeals at the College Level."

Before appealing a grade, students should be aware of the following conditions established by the Franklin College Bylaws:

1. A student may appeal a grade if, and only if, he or she is able to demonstrate that the grade was based on factors other than a fair assessment of the student's academic performance in the course.

2. The standards by which grades are assigned, the number and relative weight of assignments on which grades are based, and decisions to allow students to make up or retake missed examinations or assignments, are not grounds for appeal.

Incompletes

The University assigns certain grades that are not computed in the grade point average. The Incomplete ("I") is one of these. It indicates that students have completed almost all of the course work satisfactorily but were unable to meet the full requirements of the course for reasons beyond their control.

When assigning Incompletes, instructors will explain in writing what students must do to finish the course. Students who receive Incompletes may have no longer than three semesters to complete all remaining work satisfactorily. Instructors can require that students complete work in a shorter period of time. If an "I" is not removed after three terms (including Summer), it changes to an "F." Incompletes are assigned sparingly and at the discretion of the instructor and the Director of the First-year Composition Program when a small amount of essential work remains. An "I" is never assigned prior to mid-semester or for the purpose of allowing students to repeat courses.

General Grading Weights

The meaning of grades is defined generally in the undergraduate version of the *University of Georgia Bulletin*: http://www.bulletin.uga.edu/.

The meaning of grades according to the First-year Composition Program and grading rubric is defined as follows:

C	Competent / Credible / Complete	(70-79)
B	Skillful / Persuasive	(80-89)
A	Distinctive	(90-100)
D	Ineffective	(60-69)
F	Extremely Ineffective	(<60)
WF	Withdrew, failing	
WP	Withdrew, passing	

See the discussion of the FYC Grading Rubric below for more information about grading procedures.

Plus/Minus Grading

Plus and minus grades are assigned only to a student's final average for the course. For the final course grade, the numerical range for each plus/minus grade is as follows:

A	4.0	(92-100)
A-	3.7	(90-91)
B+	3.3	(88-89)
B	3.0	(82-87)
B-	2.7	(80-81)
C+	2.3	(78-79)
C	2.0	(70-77)
C-	1.7	(68-69)
D	1.0	(60-67)
F	0.0	(<60)

CHAPTER FOUR

Using <emma>™ in the First-year Composition Program

4

A Brief Introduction to <emma>™

All students in First-year Composition (FYC) at UGA use the program's open-source, digital learning space, <emma>™.

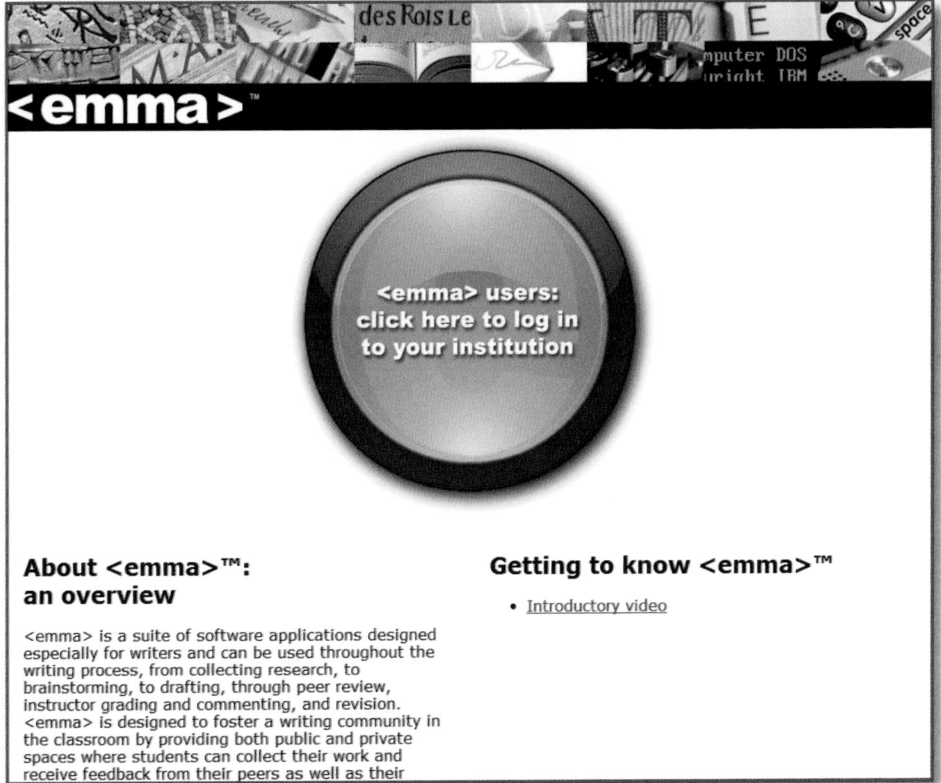

The <emma>™ Home Page

Designed especially for students and instructors, <emma>™ is a suite of software applications that can be used throughout the composition process, from collecting research, brainstorming, and drafting through peer review, revision, and instructor grading and commenting. <emma>™ collects and organizes many of the tools useful for multimodal composition within an environment that is designed to foster a classroom learning community by providing both public and private spaces where students can collect their work and receive feedback from their peers and instructor.

For example, the Notes and Research tool provides a private space where students can generate ideas and collect and begin organizing their notes and information about their sources. When you are ready to begin the drafting process, use the Notes and Research tool to generate an outline from your research notes, including a preliminary Works Cited list. Then copy-and-paste your draft text into a document created using a word processor such as OpenOffice or save it as a new eDocument. Students can make these drafts available to the class for peer review or maintain them as private documents viewable only by themselves or their instructor.

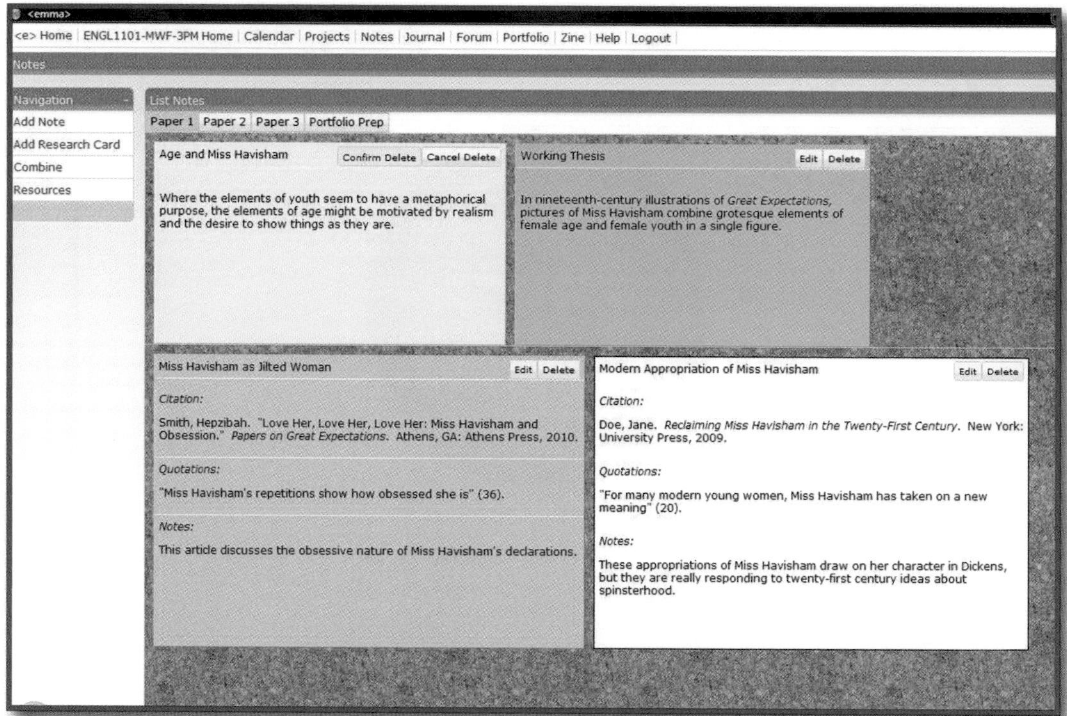

The Notes and Research Space

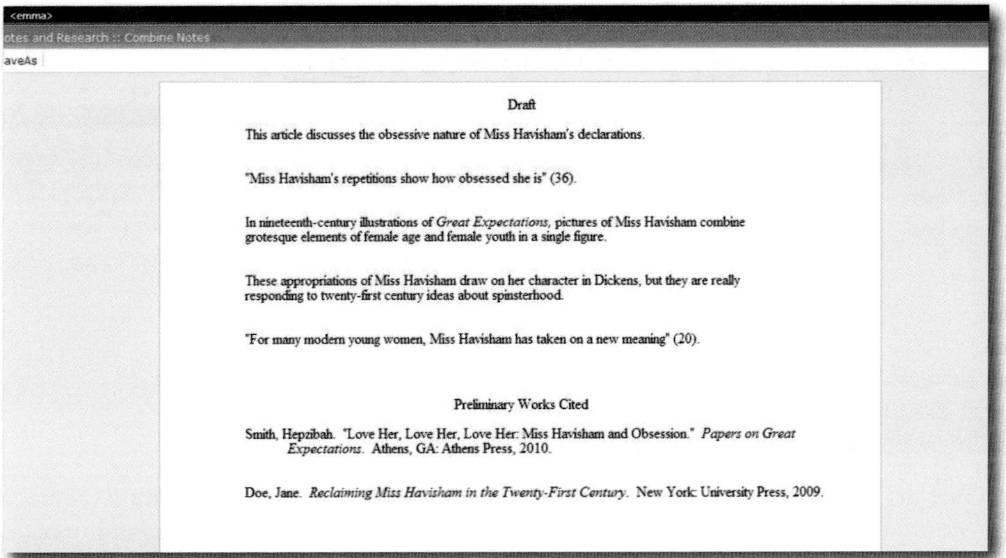

<emma>

otes and Research :: Combine Notes

aveAs

Draft

This article discusses the obsessive nature of Miss Havisham's declarations.

"Miss Havisham's repetitions show how obsessed she is" (36).

In nineteenth-century illustrations of *Great Expectations,* pictures of Miss Havisham combine grotesque elements of female age and female youth in a single figure.

These appropriations of Miss Havisham draw on her character in Dickens, but they are really responding to twenty-first century ideas about spinsterhood.

"For many modern young women, Miss Havisham has taken on a new meaning" (20).

Preliminary Works Cited

Smith, Hepzibah. "Love Her, Love Her, Love Her: Miss Havisham and Obsession." *Papers on Great Expectations.* Athens, GA: Athens Press, 2010.

Doe, Jane. *Reclaiming Miss Havisham in the Twenty-First Century.* New York: University Press, 2009.

From Notes to Draft

The Comment function operates as an asynchronous chat and offers peers and instructors the opportunity to engage in an ongoing discussion of a draft-in-progress. For more focused peer and instructor review, students and instructors can use word-processor templates to integrate feedback offline and then upload the reviewed draft.

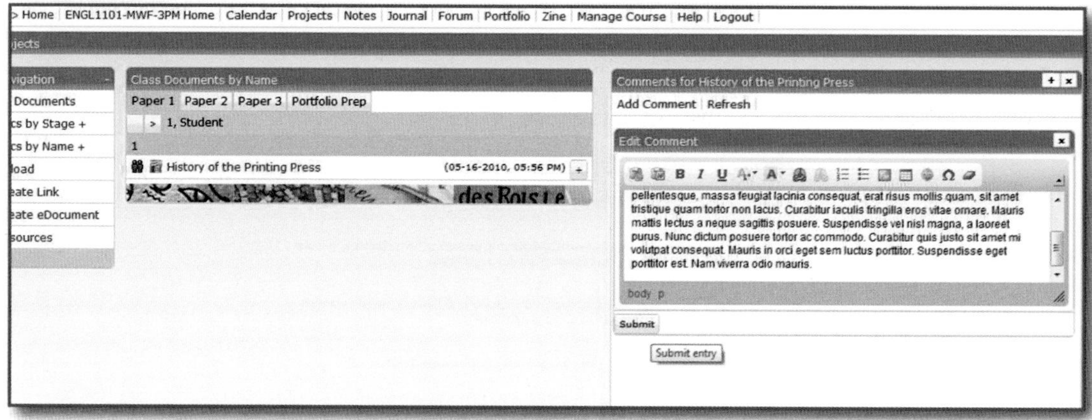

Draft with Online Comments

Once drafts have been peer and/or instructor reviewed and uploaded, <emma>™ combines and transforms the reviewed drafts into a single document that displays additional useful content, such as: 1) information drawn from *The St. Martin's Handbook;* 2) document trees to assist the writer with visualizing the structure of her argument; and 3) information about the relationship between instructor comments and the contents of a grading rubric.

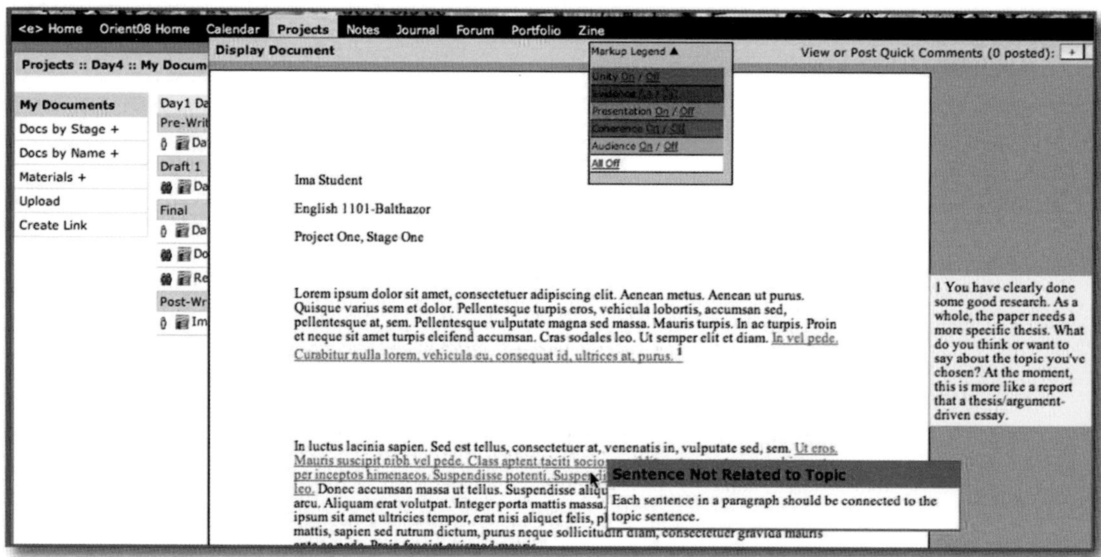

The Completed Document, with Helpful Information

The Journal tool offers students a private, informal space in which they can begin the writing process by reflecting on class readings and discussion. Journal entries are viewable only by the student and the instructor.

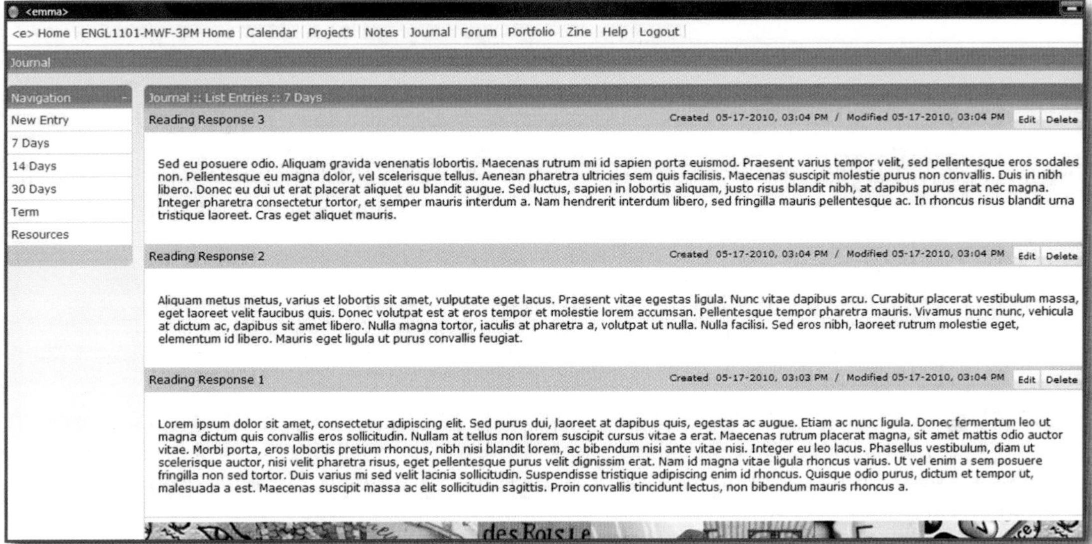

The <emma>™ Journal

The Forum tool is a public writing space where instructors and students can exchange ideas about readings, class discussions, and the composition process. Forum postings are viewable by everyone enrolled in the class.

The Forum Space in <emma>™

For your final assignment in the course portfolio, you will collect exhibits of your work and reflections upon the composition process and other activities in your classroom learning community for your <emma>™ electronic portfolio. (See below for more information about the ePortfolio.)

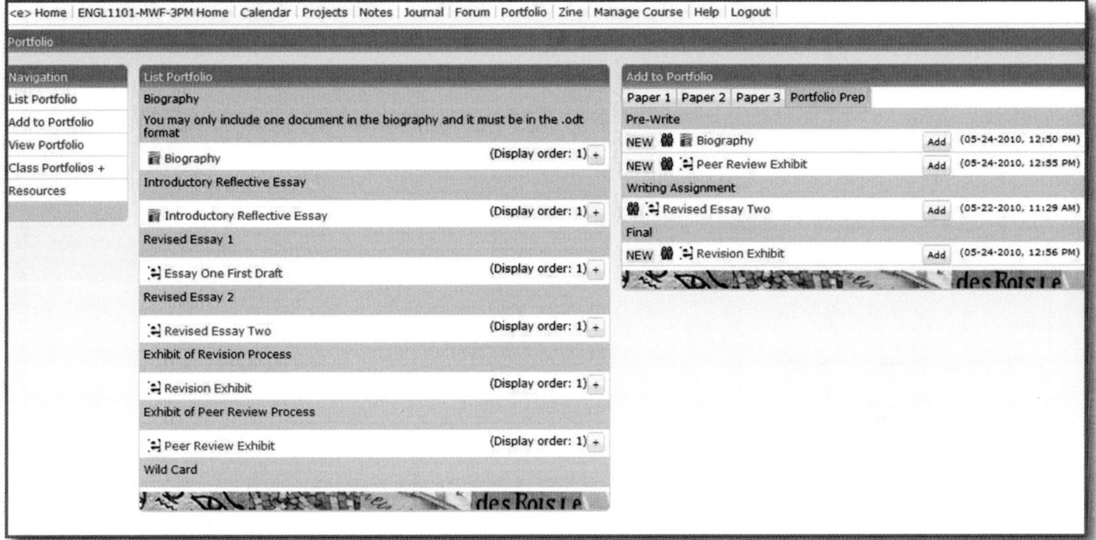

Your <emma>™ ePortfolio

Where the Portfolio provides a space for individual students to display their best work, class Zines offer collaborative workspaces that showcase the abilities of the class as a whole.

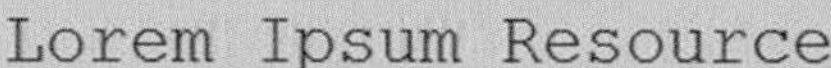

This zine is about all things lorem ipsum, including the history of the text and its modern uses.

Lorem ipsum
dolor sit amet, consectetur adipisicing elit, sed do eiusmod tempor incididunt ut labore et dolore magna aliqua. Ut enim ad minim veniam, quis nostrud exercitation ullamco laboris nisi ut aliquip ex ea commodo consequat. Duis aute irure dolor in reprehenderit in voluptate velit esse cillum dolore eu fugiat nulla pariatur. Excepteur sint occaecat cupidatat non proident, sunt in culpa qui officia deserunt mollit anim id est laborum.

Contents:

The History of Lorem Ipsum

Before it was filler, it was a text. The text of lorem ipsum dates back to 45 BC.

A Class Zine Showcases the Skills of the <emma>™ Writing Community

Now, some technical information: Because FYC at UGA is interested in fostering an open and accessible learning community, <emma>™ uses the ODF standard, which has been adopted by the International Standards Organization (ISO) and the Organization for the Advancement of Structured Information Standards (OASIS). Unlike files saved in proprietary formats—such as .doc, .wpd, or the newer .docx—that can be created and accessed only by using relatively expensive word processing software (e.g., Microsoft Word or Corel WordPerfect), .odt files can be created and accessed using a number of free software applications.

In addition, because <emma>™ has been designed as a multimodal composition platform, it accepts MP3, JPEG, and PDF files, as well as ODF files containing multimedia elements such as images and hyperlinks. As long as they do not exceed the 4MB size limit, you can upload and access files in these additional multimedia formats. Depending upon the file format and the browser you are using, these files may be accessed within the browser and <emma>™ or you may need to download them.

<emma>™ does accept files in .doc, .docx., .ppt, and .pptx. Files in these formats can only be downloaded and accessed using the proprietary software with which they were created. Your instructor may or may not accept assignments in these formats over the course of the semester. **For the final portfolio, however, only files in open formats (eDocs, ODF, PDF, MP3, JPEG, SWF, FLV), which are generally accessible using a web browser and standard plug-ins or system software, should be submitted as portfolio artifacts. Microsoft Word documents (.doc or .docx format) will not be accepted in the ePortfolio.**

OpenOffice, an open-source word processing application that uses the ODF standard, has been installed on all of the computers in the <emma>™ Lab (Park 117) and the Miller Learning Center (MLC). Students who have personal computers and would like to use them to create documents will need to make sure that they have downloaded and installed a word processor, such as OpenOffice (www.openoffice.org), that uses the ODF standard, or they need to ensure that their proprietary word processing software can access and create ODF files. **All final drafts of ODF files created for inclusion in the portfolio should be created using OpenOffice or converted to PDF to ensure that document formatting is retained in the browser to the greatest extent possible.** Students and instructors should remain aware, though, that the conversion from ODF to XHTML may occasionally result in minor formatting changes and make allowances for them. Students can get help with personal word processing solutions in the <emma>™ Lab.

In addition to using ODF-compliant word-processing software, students should use one of the following browsers to access <emma>™: Mozilla Firefox, Google Chrome, or Apple Safari. Like OpenOffice, Firefox has been installed on all of the computers in the <emma>™ Lab and the Miller Learning Center (MLC). Firefox, Chrome, and Safari are all freely available for download from the web (www.mozilla.org, www.google.com/chrome/, and www.apple.com/safari/). Students can get help with downloading and installing these programs on their personal computers from the <emma>™ Lab.

To get an <emma>™ account, you can call up the <emma>™ homepage (www.emma.uga.edu) in an <emma>™-compatible browser and click on the big green button that says, "<emma>™ users: click here to log in to your institution." After selecting "The University of Georgia," you can click on "Create Account/Reset Password" and <emma>™ will walk you through all of the steps necessary to create an account. Once you have an <emma>™ account, you can logon and enroll in a class from your personal <emma>™ homepage by clicking on "Enroll" in the left-hand toolbar.

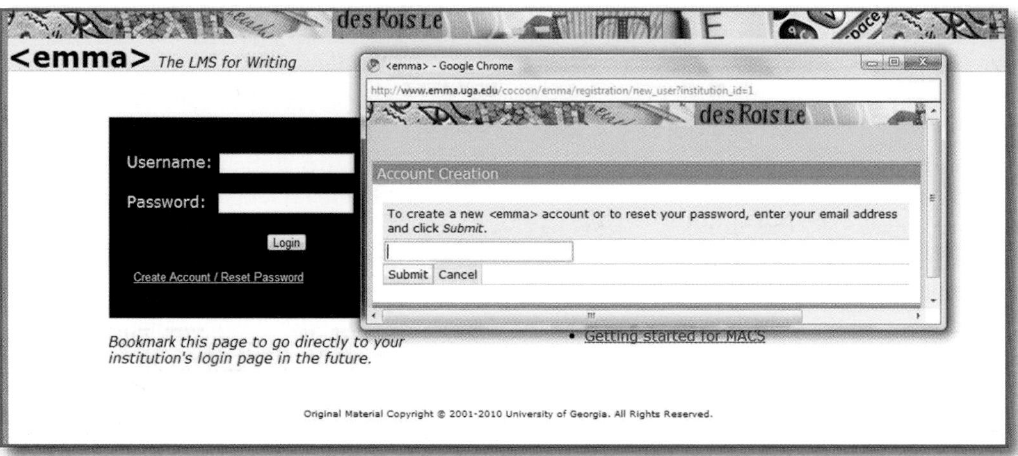

Creating your <emma>™ Account

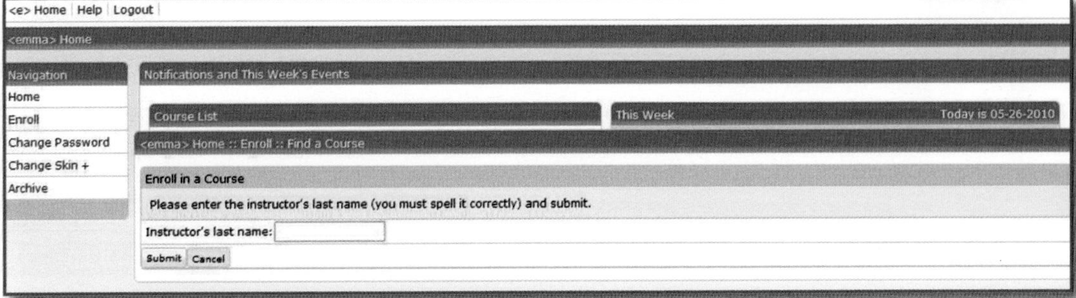

Enrolling in a Course

From your <emma>™ homepage, you can also change the look and feel of <emma>™ by using the "Change Skin" feature and change your password from the default password generated when you created your account to something you will remember more easily. The homepage also provides notices and updates of upcoming events and assignments for all of the classes in which your instructor is using <emma>™.

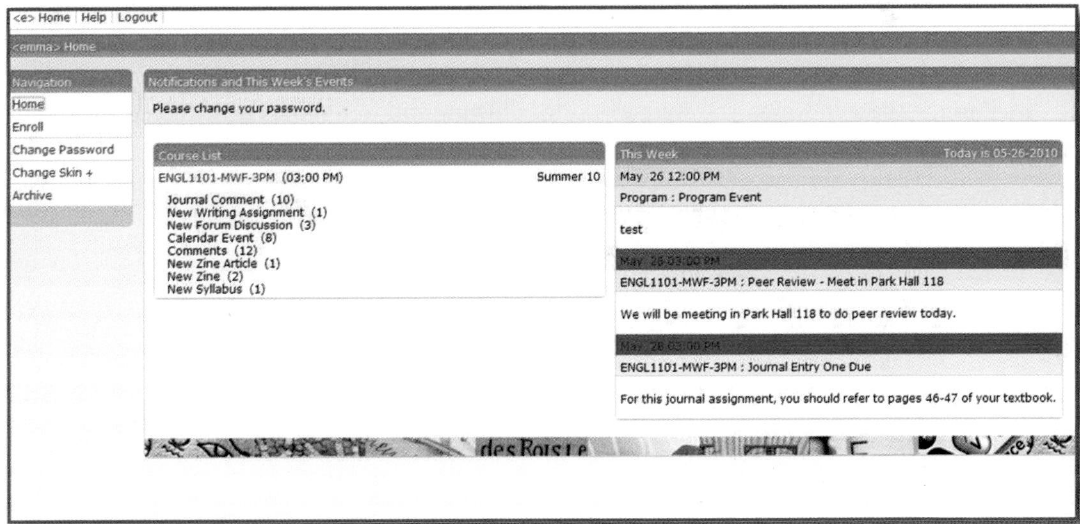

<emma>™ Keeps you Posted about Upcoming Events

Once you are enrolled in a course, you can access your class by clicking on the name of the class on the <emma>™ homepage, which will take you to Course Home. Course Home gives you a quick snapshot of upcoming events for the week and a Class Roll where students can find instructor and peer e-mail addresses.

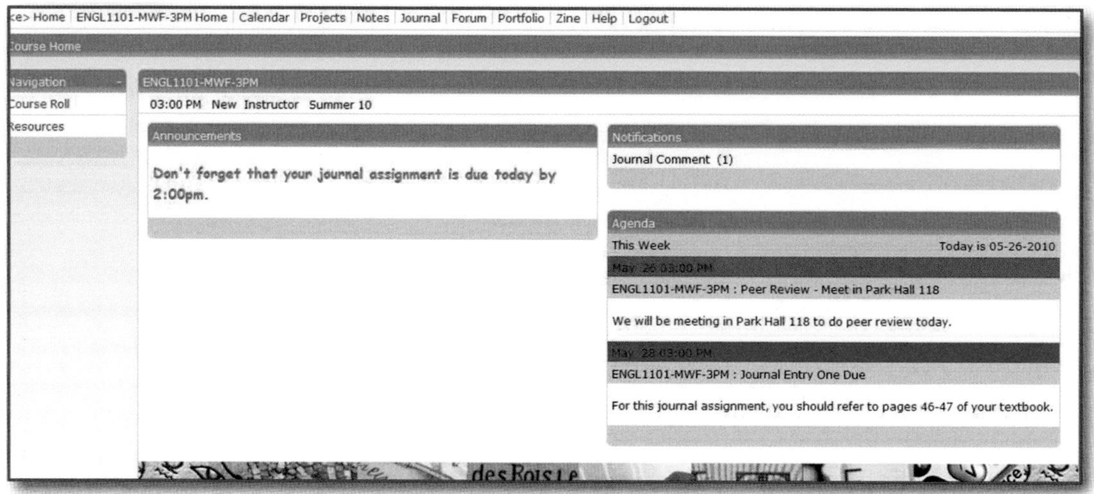

Course Home for your FYC Class in <emma>™

From anywhere in an <emma>™ course students can access course materials such as the syllabus, writing assignments, readings, handouts, and the *St. Martin's Handbook* by clicking on Resources in the left-hand toolbar. Closing the Resources dialog returns you back to the space in which you were working, allowing you to resume right where you left off.

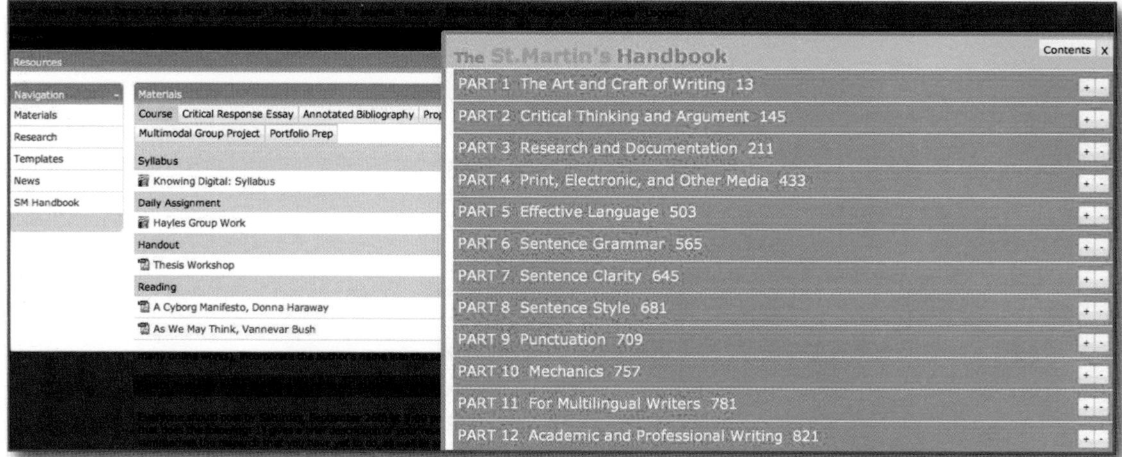

<emma>™ Provides Intuitive Access to Important Resources

<emma>™ organizes writing assignments into Projects. Instructors can associate readings, handouts and other resources with these Projects. By selecting Projects from the navigation bar at the top of the screen, students can access all of their own work related to that Project. This is also how students can find the work that their peers have made accessible for peer review.

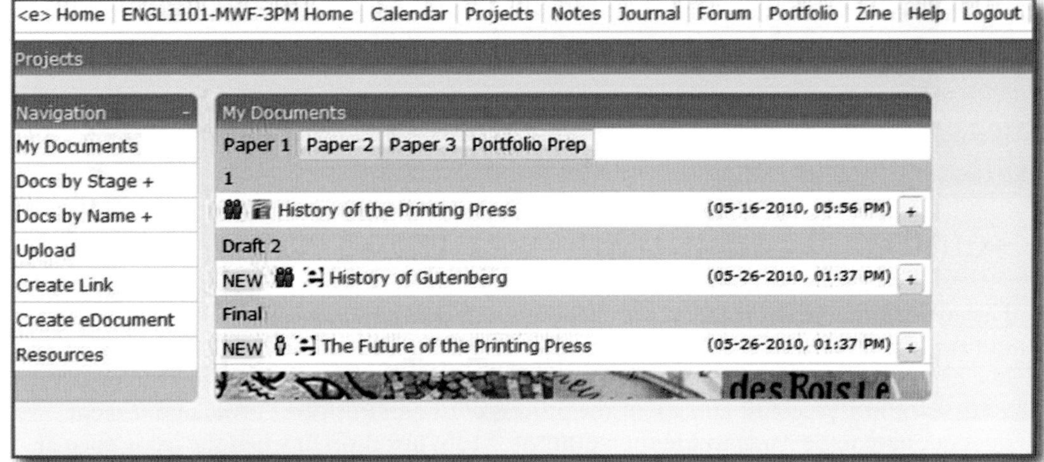

<emma>™ Organizes your Work According to Projects for the Course

The navigation bar also provides students with access to the <emma>™ Calendar, their Notes and Research, the Journal, the Forum, class Zines, and the Portfolio. Instructors can use the Calendar to notify students of daily assignments, important due dates, and other events.

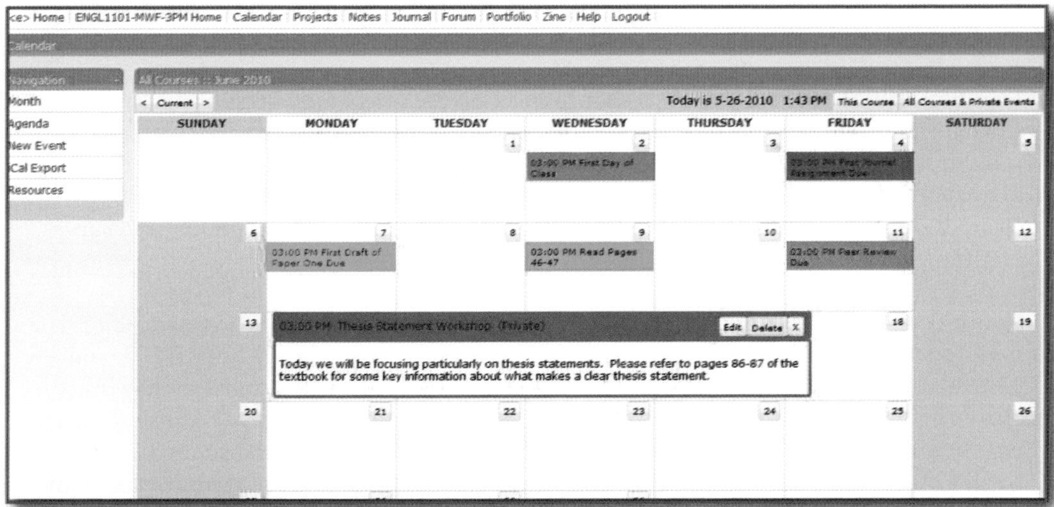

<emma>™ Helps You Keep Track of Assignments and Due Dates

This has been a quick tour of <emma>™. You will learn more during your <emma>™ orientation and as you use <emma>™ throughout the semester. You can also find more comprehensive information in the <emma>™ Help documentation, and get assistance with using <emma>™ from the <emma>™ Support Team in the <emma>™ Lab.

The <emma>™ Lab, where you can bring any of your <emma>™ questions and problems, is in

PARK HALL 117

<emma>™ LAB AND SUPPORT TEAM (FROGS)

First-year Composition students are encouraged to take advantage of the <emma>™ Lab in Park 117. There, on any week day during regular business hours, you will find at least one member of the <emma>™ support staff to answer any questions you may have about your <emma>™ account and about the process of using <emma>™. An appointment does not have to be made to use the <emma>™ Lab; just drop in when the lab is open at a time most convenient for you.

The <emma>™ Lab is staffed by First-year Composition teachers who use <emma>™ in their classrooms and who often lead <emma>™ orientations at the beginning of the semester and administer course and instructor evaluations near the end of the semester. Generically, individuals on the <emma>™ support staff are referred to as "Frogs" –the reason being, historically, that technical support personnel "eat" "bugs." One can refer to the person occupying the desk at the front of the room as a "frog" without necessarily insulting him or her, provided that the tone used is not ironic.

Sign In: The <emma>™ Lab has a sign-in sheet on the desk at the front of the room that students must sign before using the facilities. All one needs to know for the sign-in sheet is his or her name, his or her teacher's last name, and the time. This sheet is for the benefit of everyone, as it helps the First-year Composition Office track how many students are using the <emma>™ Lab and when, and in so doing it ensures future funding and support for the lab.

Printing: There is also a printer available in the <emma>™ Lab that First-year Composition students may use to print out materials necessary for their ENGL 1101, 1102, and 1102m classes. Students should be advised, however, that materials printed for any other classes will not be made available to them after printing and will be recycled, instead. It is necessary to enforce this rule because the lab is funded through a special student fee, paid by all FYC students and only by FYC students, that allows use of these print resources for First-year Composition-related purposes only.

Lab Policies:

- Out of respect for others and the work they are doing in the lab, please conduct cell phone conversations outside of the room;
- No food or drink in the lab;

- First-year Composition business takes precedence over any other for the lab computers. If you are not working on a project for your composition class, please allow students working with <emma> ™ primary use of the lab's equipment.

Open Source Tools: Apart from Firefox, OpenOffice, and the usual office tools, a number of other open source tools have been added to the desktops of most of the lab computers. Three items of note are:

- Audacity, for sound editing/recording and mixing (be sure to bring your own headphones and microphone);
- Komposer, a web editor; and
- Gimp, a photoshop tool.

Recycling bins: At times, the <emma> ™ Lab can generate lots of paper. Please try to remember to recycle what you do not need in one of the bins at the front of the room.

CHAPTER FIVE

Evaluation of Essays in the First-year Composition Program

5

What Do Teachers Want?

Because all writing, no matter how personal, attempts to communicate with some audience, writing is a social art. And all writers—whether students writing to develop their skills, amateurs writing to satisfy personal ambition, or professionals writing to support themselves—need to get some reaction to their writing. One form of reaction students get is from peer evaluation. By critiquing one another's papers constructively in workshops, student writers gain immediate insight into the effectiveness of their argumentation and prose. Students also receive comments on graded essays from their English teachers.

How teachers grade an essay should interest all students. First, they should understand that no exact correlation exists between the number of marks on a paper and the grade that paper receives. An essay does not begin as a "100" and then lose points as the teacher finds errors. Rather, the teacher evaluates the paper according to its effectiveness in communicating with an intended audience. Effective communication involves both mechanical correctness and rhetorical skill. Students who fail to distinguish between these two concerns may mistakenly believe that English teachers look only for misspelled words and grammar and punctuation errors when grading papers. Although mechanical errors can seriously damage the overall effectiveness of a piece of writing, to write well students must do more than merely rid papers of mechanical errors. Effective communication depends primarily on rhetorical concerns; in other words, how effectively does the writing assignment being evaluated meet the needs of a particular audience and accomplish a particular purpose?

The grading rubric used for our First-year Composition program recognizes that "good" writing is embedded in a particular situation. For example, if students are writing an informational essay on nuclear energy for someone who knows little about the subject, they might decide to explain basic principles and processes, using simple comparisons to familiar things (content); to proceed in their explanation from the simplest to the most complex process or principle (organization); and to employ a neutral tone and use ordinary terms rather than a specialist's jargon (style). This example reveals that the "best" content, organization, and style depend on the essay's topic, purpose, and reader. Our grading rubric evaluates the elements of content, organization, and style as a whole and with respect to their overall rhetorical effectiveness and designates essays as Competent, Skillful, Distinctive, or Ineffective.

Finally, from these remarks, students should understand that the teacher weighs a number of factors in assigning a grade to a paper. Depending on the particular assignment, the teacher may decide to weigh one factor more heavily than others. In the first paper, for example, the teacher may be most concerned that students develop clear unity or thoroughly researched evidence and least concerned about the essay's audience awareness. But later in the semester, after the class has studied audience awareness, the teacher may weigh both factors. Students should also expect grading standards to become more stringent as the class progresses through the semester and as they move through the two First-year Composition courses.

What Grades on Essays Mean

The meaning of grades is defined generally in the undergraduate version of the University of Georgia Bulletin: http://www.bulletin.uga.edu/.

The meaning of grades according to the First-year Composition Program and grading rubric is defined as follows:

C	Competent / Credible / Complete	(70-79)
B	Skillful / Persuasive	(80-89)
A	Distinctive	(90-100)
D	Ineffective	(60-69)
F	Extremely Ineffective	(<60)
WF	Withdrew, failing	
WP	Withdrew, passing	

Plus/Minus Grading

Plus and minus grades are assigned only to a student's final average for the course. For the final course grade, the numerical range for each plus/minus grade is as follows:

A	4.0	(92-100)
A-	3.7	(90-91)
B+	3.3	(88-89)
B	3.0	(82-87)
B-	2.7	(80-81)
C+	2.3	(78-79)
C	2.0	(70-77)
C-	1.7	(68-69)
D	1.0	(60-67)
F	0.0	(<60)

Grading Rubric

Here is the actual rubric that your teacher will use when evaluating your essays and often will encourage you to use when critiquing your peers' essays and making judgments about your own work.

Student's Name____________________ **Teacher** ____________________

Paper #____ **Special Assignment Requirements:** ____________________

Conference__________

"Enter a pertinent quote here." (Teachers can self-select)

Writing Center__________

_____ **Competent/Credible/Complete**

If you meet these first three standards, you are writing competently and you will earn a grade of "C." (70-79)

1. **Unity**
   - Contains a center of gravity, a unifying and controlling purpose, a thesis or claim, which is maintained throughout the paper.
   - Organizes writing around a thesis or according to the organizational requirements of the particular assignment (e.g., summary, narrative, argument, analysis, description, etc.)
2. **Evidence/Development**
   - Develops appropriate, logical, and relevant supporting detail and/or evidence.
   - Includes more specific, concrete evidence (or details) than opinion or abstract, general commentary.
3. **Presentation and Design**
   - Follows SMH guidelines for Standard English grammar, punctuation, usage, and documentation.
   - Meets your teacher's (or the MLA's) and the First-year Composition program's requirements for length and/or format.

_____ **Skillful/Persuasive**

If you meet all of the competency standards above and, in addition, achieve coherence and exhibit audience awareness, you are writing skillfully and you will earn a grade of "B." (80-89)

4. **Coherence**
   - Uses words and sentences, rhythm and phrasing, variations and transitions, concreteness and specificity to *reveal and emphasize the relationship* between evidence and thesis.
   - Explains how, why, or in what way the evidence/detail provided supports the claim/ point /thesis/topic ideas.
   - Incorporates evidence from outside sources smoothly, appropriately, and responsibly.
5. **Audience Awareness**
   - Demonstrates a sense that the writer knows what s/he's doing and is addressing real people.
   - Reflects a respect for values that influence ethos (e.g., common ground, trustworthiness, careful research).

_____ **Distinctive**

If you meet all of the competency standards, achieve coherence and exhibit audience awareness, and, in addition, demonstrate a mastery of one or more features of superior writing, you are writing distinctively and you will earn a grade of "A." (90-100)

6. **Distinction**
   - Your writing stands out because of one or more of the following characteristics: complexity, originality, seamless coherence, extraordinary control, sophistication in thought, recognizable voice, compelling purpose, imagination, insight, thoroughness, and/or depth.

Essay Grade ______ **+/- Points for special assignment requirements** ______ = **Final Grade**

_____ **Ineffective**

If your paper does not meet competency standards, either because you have minor problems in all three competence areas (1-3 above) or major problems in one or two competence areas, you will earn a grade of "D" (60-69) or "F" (<60), and you should schedule a conference with your teacher.

University of Georgia First-year Composition Grading Rubric 2010-11 5/15/10

Using the Grading Rubric's Vocabulary

We use the FYC Grading Rubric throughout our First-year Composition program because it helps teachers, tutors, students, and sometimes advisors, parents, and administrators to understand what our program values and looks for in student writing. Many teachers use an electronic version of this rubric and mark essays with coded electronic tags and inserted comments, while other teachers clip or staple a paper copy of the rubric, along with their handwritten notes, directly to student papers. Whether paper or electronic—whichever form of the rubric they use—teachers depend on the standard rubric's language to guide their evaluation of student papers, while students must depend to some degree on the rubric's language to understand their teachers' comments. Finally, the rubric's common vocabulary helps students comment on one another's work and to make judgments about their own essays. The Rubric helps to keep all parties on the same page!

In order to help students (and teachers) use the Rubric most effectively, here we discuss some of the key terms:

Competent/Credible/Complete

In order to receive a passing and satisfactory grade of "C," an essay needs to meet the three principal criteria of Unity, Evidence/Development, and Presentation and Design.

1. Unity = Staying on topic and providing structure

⇒"Contains a center of gravity, a unifying and controlling purpose, a thesis or claim, which is maintained throughout the paper."

First-year compositions can be organized in many different ways. Papers may have an implicit or explicit thesis, or they may simply have a unifying purpose or theme. In any unified paper, however, **every sentence and every word will contribute in some way towards the exposition and development of the "main" idea**.

Notice, too, that at the level of competency "unity" does not require a particularly complex, clever, or imaginative thesis, nor does unity require strong coherence. For example, if my thesis were "cats are annoying," unity would only require that every sentence be somehow relevant to the "topic" (i.e., "cats") and the "comment" (i.e., "are annoying"), the two elements that the *St. Martin's Handbook* defines as central to a thesis. Teachers may need to read between the lines a bit in evaluating a paper for unity; peer review can also provide useful feedback to writers about the unity of their essays. For instance, sometimes an apparently unrelated comment, such as "Cats often have long, fluffy fur," may need just a word or two (perhaps a word or two about shedding, allergies and long, fluffy fur on couches!) to firmly demonstrate unity.

⇒ "Organizes writing around a thesis or according to the organizational requirements of the particular assignment (e.g., summary, narrative, argument, analysis, description, etc.)"

Simply put, to "organize writing around a thesis" or **other central point** means that the essay reveals, under examination, **an overall organizational plan or strategy**. Could this essay be outlined? Does it have a definite beginning, middle, and end? A clearly organized essay might use logical, spatial, chronological, or even associational order—but the strategy will suit the topic and the purpose of the paper.

2. Evidence/Development = Providing support (examples, details, or specifics)

⇒ "Develops appropriate, logical, and relevant supporting detail and/or evidence."

This criterion asks you to note whether the writer uses examples and/or other evidence to support his/her argument, position, or idea and whether that evidence is fairly used, accurate, and relevant. Depending on the kind of essay you have been assigned, good evidence may include anecdotes, images, descriptions, and dialogue or primary and secondary sources, graphs, and charts; typically, evidence will include quotations from a variety of sources—often the texts read in class. You are evaluating the **quality of evidence** and sources here. Did the writer use the evidence accurately and fairly? Or to give another example, was the scene described with concrete details?

⇒ "Includes more specific, concrete evidence (quotations, interviews, charts, statistics, details, description, observation, and dialogue) than opinion or abstract, general commentary."

This criterion asks you to gauge **quantity of evidence**. Has the writer spent most of the essay making general statements and assertions about the topic? Or, instead, has he/she used most of his/her words and sentences to clarify and define the argument, giving examples and explaining connections to assertions? How many opinion statements are there versus how many examples/quotations/details? Typically, you would hope to find a good deal more evidence than opinion. On the other hand, does the writer string together many quotations and facts into lists or very lengthy quoted passages? Is there **too much** unincorporated and unexplained evidence?

3. Presentation and Design = Correctness and formatting issues

⇒ "Follows guidelines for standard English grammar, punctuation, usage, and documentation."

To meet this criterion, here is a general rule of thumb: To pass at the level of Competency, a paper should contain 2 or fewer major errors + 4 or fewer minor errors/250-word page, OR 8 or fewer minor errors/250-word page. All the major errors have to do with either sentence boundary recognition or Standard English grammar issues. For our purposes, the major errors are:

Comma Splice
Fragment
Fused Sentence
Subject/Verb Agreement
Pronoun/Antecedent Agreement.

All other errors are considered minor errors. If a student's paper has more errors than the standard described above, the paper is not meeting competency guidelines.

Remember, however, that this standard is just a guideline. Simply lacking a large number of errors does not necessarily make an essay "Competent" or passing. As we point out in the Introduction to this section: "An essay does not begin as a '100' and then lose points as the teacher finds errors."

⇒ "Meets your teacher's (or the MLA's) and the First-year Composition Program's requirements for length and/or format."

The standard format and documentation requirements for First-year Composition follow those for MLA formatting. Teachers may have special requirements, which may include things like specialized or alternative style sheets, images, graphs, particular fonts, minimum word counts, bibliographies, appendices, notes, abstracts, etc.

EXAMPLE:

Here is an excerpt from one of the 2008-2009 Barnett Award Essays showing how a student working at the Distinctive level, excels in all three Competency requirements. These opening paragraphs, which lay out the background and set up the argument of the essay, show excellent unity, with a strong thesis and a clearly signaled paragraph structure. All sentences are on topic and linked to the thesis. The student also begins to introduce a wide variety of specific and high-quality supporting evidence and does a good job of integrating these sources into her own compelling discussion. In addition to this writer's careful documentation, the paper has been correctly and thoroughly revised, edited, and proofread.

"A system that will take life must first give justice."
—Former ABA President John J. Curtin, Jr.

Our human lives are brief. Once taken, they can never be retrieved. Therefore, if a life has to be blotted out, the justification for this action must be legitimate. An unwarranted execution is equivalent to an unjust murder. The Law of Parties, section 7.02 of the Texas Penal Code, states that codefendants may be held criminally responsible for each other's actions if they acted as co-conspirators, even if one defendant commits a spontaneous felony without his codefendant's consent (Penal). In layman's terms, the Law of Parties upholds the view of guilt by association. This is the law under which Jeffery Wood has been convicted.

In 1996, two men, Daniel Reneau and Jeffery Wood, were convicted on the charge of premeditated homicide for the murder of Texaco Gas Station Clerk Kris Keeran during a staged robbery in Kerrville, Texas (Fears 2A). Interestingly, however, Wood was not even in the gas station at the time of the shooting. Rather, he was anxiously waiting in the getaway car while Reneau stormed into the gas station to rob the station's safe (Fears 2A). When Keeran failed to respond quickly enough to Reneau's demands, Reneau shot him with a .22-caliber handgun (Fears 2A). Hearing the gunfire, Wood ran into the building. It was at this point that Reneau, holding Wood at gunpoint, threatened both Wood and his family as he ordered him to remove both the safe and surveillance camera (McCann). Eventually, both Reneau and Wood were sentenced to capital punishment, with Reneau being executed by lethal injection in 2002 (McCann, McKinley 12A).

Currently, Wood resides on death row awaiting his final hearing in either February or March of this coming year after being granted *moratoria* (McKinley 12A). He was found guilty simply because of his involvement with Reneau in this robbery. Jeff Wood, who has been found mentally unstable, neither had a weapon, nor shot or gravely injured anyone. Yet, he has been condemned to death under Texas law. The argument being presented here does not dispute the legality or morality of capital punishment, but of the Texas legal system. The Law of Parties has a deleterious effect on the Texan citizenry because it totally disregards the Eighth Amendment to the United States Constitution: because this law can be misapplied to punish those, even to execute those, not responsible for criminal actions, it leads to cruel and unusual punishment.

Capital punishment is reserved for those who commit first-degree murder. The only crime that Wood committed was confiscating the safe and surveillance-camera tape and driving the getaway car. Therefore, to execute him is a violation of the Eighth Amendment of the United States Constitution, which states that "cruel and unusual punishment [shall not be] inflicted." This opinion is upheld by four Supreme Court cases and one state court case: *Coker v. Georgia* (1977), *Enmund v. Florida* (1982), *Kennedy v. Louisiana* (2008), *Atkins v. Virginia* (2002), and *The Texas Department of Community Affairs v. Burdine* (1984).

Excerpted from: "Death by Association: The Jeffery Wood Case"
Student: Stephanie Ryals
Teacher: Annalee Edmondson ENGL 1101

Skillful/Persuasive

In order to reach the level of a "Skillful/Persuasive" paper, an argument must have two additional qualities: Coherence and Audience Awareness

4. Coherence = The "Flow"

⇒ "Uses words and sentences, rhythm and phrasing, variations and transitions, concreteness and specificity to reveal and emphasize the relationship between evidence and thesis."

In general, while students can achieve unity by creating a strong thesis and staying on topic, they create coherence by focusing their reader's attention on the *relationship* between thesis and evidence (or theme and detail). Creating Coherence is about **controlling emphasis**.

Students may use diction to emphasize the thesis-to-evidence connections by choosing words carefully, by repeating key words and phrases, by avoiding the repetition of unimportant words and phrases, and by using transitional phrases accurately. Writers can also use syntax, that is, sentence structure, to direct emphasis by varying sentence structures, by using syntactical effects such as parallelism and antithesis, or by simply changing sentence length or reversing normal Subject-Verb-Object sentence patterns. In evaluating coherence, you can ask these questions: has the writer used syntax and diction to create links between his or her thoughts? Does the writer use transitional phrases and words frequently and accurately to help the reader move from sentence to sentence and from paragraph to paragraph? Does the writer's use of repetition, parallelism, figures of speech, and rhythm help to emphasize main points, OR does the writer's choice of diction and syntax distract the reader from main ideas?

⇒ "Explains how, why, or in what way the evidence/detail supports point/claim/thesis/topic ideas."

Writers need to include **explanations**. In fact, writers usually need to explain why each detail or item of support has been included in an essay. It is a rare bit of evidence that is so clear that it speaks for itself. Coherence develops as writers **explain how** each part of their arguments' evidence provides support for their theses.

⇒ "Incorporates evidence from outside sources smoothly, appropriately, and responsibly."

The writer will consistently incorporate quotations and references to other outside sources into her own sentences. Coherent writers move often between paraphrasing, summarizing, and brief selected quotations from different sources. Few, if any, quotations will be left "hanging" — that is, standing alone in separate sentences; instead, they will be embedded in the writer's own sentences, usually with explanatory remarks linking the quotations to the topic or thesis. Lengthy quotations, serial quotations, or long summaries rarely occur in a "Skillful" writer's essay.

EXAMPLE:

In the example below, the final paragraphs of a 2009-2010 Barnett Award paper, the writer, Darcy Lenz, traces the dysfunctional similarities in two families, the Lomans in Arthur Miller's iconic *Death of a Salesman* and the Hoovers in the recent film, *Little Miss Sunshine*, deftly weaving together her own observations from both works to develop an interesting and original thesis. The sample paragraphs below, taken from the end of her paper, demonstrate excellent coherence. While Lenz uses a wide variety of sources, she nevertheless creates and maintains a clear emphasis on her own position by repeating key words, using transitional elements, varying her syntax, integrating explanations into her source material, and by using many other organizing and directing elements to control emphasis, such as careful word choice, clear topic sentences, helpful definitions, and summarizing statements.

> The remainder of the play exposes the tragic results of aspiring to one man's standards of perfection, with each character demonstrating a personal response to Willy's impact. As an adult, Happy seeks compensation for affection denied to him in youth through keeping company with a wide variety of women, persistently ignorant of his and his family's state of crisis. Linda, who at least realizes that "attention must be paid" to Willy's increasing incompetency, remains blinded by her love for her husband and simply cannot bear to "insult" him (Miller 1092, 1094). Though Biff powerfully desires honest communication between his relatives, the tendencies towards irresponsibility and stealing that he develops in adolescence persistently haunt him. Rather than exhibiting any growth whatsoever, Miller's tragic hero, Willy Loman, falls deeper into delusion. Even in the midst of this confused salesman's suicide – Willy's final attempt to make success for the Lomans — the family cannot reach a peaceful consensus as to whether Willy's pristine dream is "the only dream [one] can have" (Miller 1131).
>
> The Lomans spend years complying with Willy's expectations; contrastingly, most members of the Hoover household overtly ridicule Richard's thirst for perfection. The crucial exception is Olive who, in her youthful innocence, cannot yet form her own opinions and consequently looks to her guardians for total guidance. As her father serves as a "teacher, role modeler, and socializer who demonstrate[s] . . . reward[s]s, punish[es], and otherwise shape[s]" Olive, she develops an overwhelming fear of failing (Masten and Shaffer 12). Though the rest of the family is not so easily influenced, they lack any form of unity and coexist in a state of mass confusion "trying to make sense of the world and find a secure and rational place in it" (Laurier). Uncertainty goads family member to construct walls or "boundaries" between themselves and the other family members (Conoley 4). While to an extent boundaries may exist within any ordinary family, the borders marking each Hoover's territory are exceptionally "impermeable," preventing "information, affection, and supervision" from "flow[ing] easily between" them (Conoley 4). Though the family is not exactly enthusiastic about its impending expedition to a "prepubescent" beauty pageant, the Hoovers begin connecting as a family through adversity (Laurier).

Diverging from the disastrous outcomes in *Death of a Salesman* and *Little Miss Sunshine*, honest communication between the Hoovers leads to actual unification. As family members observe Olive dance provocatively in the "Little Miss Sunshine" pageant, they realize that their family is far from perfect, but that accepting each member as he or she is is possible. Through their comedic journey of harmonious growth, the Hoovers demonstrate that, although a family may indeed experience a constant array of problems, each member must not only love but accept the others in order to fully appreciate the joys of family. In the end, the Hoover family escapes the tragic fate of the Lomans to find their own happy ending by way of recognition and acceptance.

Despite their various divergences, both *Death of a Salesman* and *Little Miss Sunshine* attest that the dire consequences of living under false pretenses are far more harmful than being the odd family on the block. This is not to say that the father figures of either drama are wicked men by any means; they are simply befuddled about how to achieve happiness for themselves or within their families. While the "traditional" family still holds respect in modern culture, the problematic family, in turn, finds far greater acceptance than in the era of *Death of a Salesman.* Family dysfunction is actually a common source of amusement for much of today's America, as is prevalent in the hoards of reality television programs focusing on the subject (Jerry Springer, Wife Swap, etc.) and the comedic plot of *Little Miss Sunshine*. However, in an era of skyrocketing divorce rates and domestic violence, one begins to wonder at what point acceptance of family imperfection converges with approval of hollow relationships.

Excerpted from: "Father Knows Best"
Student: Darcy Lenz
Instructor: Lisa Reeves ENGL 1102

5. Audience Awareness = Writing should speak to real readers

⇒ "Demonstrates a sense that the writer knows what s/he's doing and is addressing real people."

Showing that a writer "knows what s/he's doing" means that the writer works to develop his or her credibility (ethos). He or she might mention and/or demonstrate particular knowledge or research concerning the topic, demonstrate comfort and familiarity with appropriate jargon or professional vocabularies, or simply use sound logic and clear reasoning in his or her discussion. Credibility can be, however, developed in many ways. For example, the first writer below, Macy Marie Sirmans, details her own life and background to introduce a sports' profile (see Example 1). Her perspective on the football game she profiles is grounded in her own life experience, giving readers a better idea of her authority and a "sense that the writer knows what s/he's doing." Teachers and peer reviewers can also see that a writer "knows what s/he's doing" when writers demonstrate knowledge and use appropriate, timely research such as that found in the second example, Olivia Swint's analytical essay, "Rise Against: Speaking Out Against War." In Example 2, Swint immediately establishes credibility in her introductory paragraphs by specifically referencing several primary and secondary sources.

EXAMPLES:

1. In the rural, Georgia town where I grew up, football exists beyond tradition. Every grandpa raised every daddy—who raises every son—to be a Pirate Football player, to lead community uproars on chilly, fall Friday nights in the giant stadium hollowed out in the hills of Hamilton. During the season, players cannot escape Jolly's Southern Restaurant without signing the football of a young admirer. Marquees of elementary schools and local businesses read "Go Pirates" or "Keep It Up, Boys." Garages empty and windows darken at exactly 6:30 PM, giving fans an hour to find the best seat before kickoff.

   I had the privilege to experience Pirate Spirit at its very best. During four of the team's most victorious years, my blonde, ribboned ponytail bounced on the sidelines as I threw plastic footballs in the stands after every touchdown, was hoisted high in the air for each kickoff, and kept a smile on my face regardless of the scoreboard. I was a Varsity Football Cheerleader. I loved the tradition of my small town, and I was a leader for its most rallying event.

   For many in the town, Varsity Football games were a ritual, almost a religious experience. For me, the euphoria of a Pirate game was magical. Standing on the sidelines, I had a perfect view of the profound effects that a high school football game could have on my community. Fans, cheerleaders, band members, football players, and coaches were united and emotionally inspired as time stood still, the pursuit of victory pulsing through all of our bodies.

   Excerpted from: "A Profile of Pirate Football"
   Student: Macy Marie Sirmans
   Instructor: Matthew Forsythe ENGL1101

2. The punk rock band, Rise Against, was born in Chicago, Illinois in 1999. Their first album, *The Unraveling*, was released in 2001 (Keep Music Alive). The band has since produced four albums (Rise Against: Official Site). Current band members, Tim McIlrath performing vocals, Joe Principe at bass guitar and vocals, Brandon Barnes on drums, and Zach Blair on lead guitar, follow a liberal, political ideology, according to a profile by Ryan Cooper. They have been a part of Punk Voter, and they endorse PETA, People for the Ethical Treatment of Animals, which follows the same political ideologies (Cooper). Many of their songs are about standing up to the injustices occurring in the world. Their latest album, *Appeal to Reason*, tackles issues like corporate America, the declining environment, and the war in Iraq. Lead singer, Tim McIlrath, explains that the members of Rise Against want to use their punk rock music as "a vehicle for change and awareness" ("An Interview"). Rise Against has successfully employed its music and music videos as tools to raise awareness about issues in contemporary society, specifically instances of torture that have taken place during the war in Iraq.

   Excerpted from: "Rise Against: Speaking Out Against War"
   Student: Olivia Swint
   Instructor: Caroline Bartunek ENGL1101

⇒ "Reflects a respect for values that influence ethos (e.g., common ground, trustworthiness, careful research)."

Respect for an audience and values can be shown at every level. Has the writer chosen an appropriate level of formality in his or her diction — avoiding the too formal for an audience of close friends, the too familiar with teachers or general audiences? Has the writer avoided unnecessary jargon or slang? Has the writer avoided sexist or racist language? Is the writer's choice of supporting of examples and evidence appropriate, fairly used, relevant, and judiciously applied? Does the writer show a high level of integrity about facts and correctness at every level? Does the writer implicitly and explicitly show courtesy and good will towards readers whose opinions may differ? Does the writer acknowledge counter-arguments and other positions?

The example from the 2008-2009 Barnett Awards below, written on a literary topic that deals with both religious and cultural issues, successfully negotiates this territory with careful research, abundant incorporation of sources, and a clear, but modest, analytical ethos.

EXAMPLE:

Differing characterizations of God further define the distinct purposes of Johnson's poem and the prose of Genesis. While the preacher in "The Creation" depicts God as anthropomorphic, the speaker in Genesis portrays God as regal, omnipotent, and infallible — essentially superhuman. The difference in the characterization of God is first evident in the introductory stanza of the poem and in verse one of Genesis. Although both versions establish that God exists alone in time and space, the Biblical text does not indicate that God is lonely, which is a specifically human emotion. Conversely, Johnson's text quotes God as saying, "I'm lonely – / I'll make a world" ("Creation" 3, 4). God's loneliness, coupled with the personified acts of God stepping "out on space," looking, and speaking, give human characteristics to a God who is in no way humanized in the first verse of Genesis, which omnipotently says, "In the beginning God created the heavens and the earth" (*New International Version Bible*, Gen. 1.1). Unlike the God of "The Creation," the God of Genesis does not contemplate aloud what he wants to do. Rather, he simply acts, and through this simplicity of creation, the God of Genesis brings superhuman order and premeditation to the text.

Excerpted from: "James Weldon Johnson's 'The Creation' and the Biblical Creation: A Comparison"
Student: Ellen Davis
Instructor: Liz Vasconcelos ENGL1102M

Distinctive

To earn the highly coveted grade of "A," a writer must go beyond basic criteria required for a competent essay, exceed the expectations for a skillful essay, and provide something else that gives the essay real "value added," sticks in the reader's memory, or catches her attention.

6. Distinction: A few words about distinction

⇒ "Your writing stands out because of one or more of the following characteristics: complexity, originality, seamless coherence, extraordinary control, sophistication in thought, recognizable voice, compelling purpose, imagination, insight, thoroughness, and/or depth."

No single quality reveals distinction; that's why we've listed so many possibilities. A paper should meet standards in all five of the other criteria before it is considered for "Distinction." This does not mean students' papers must necessarily **excel** in all five criteria (although many will and most will excel in 3 or more criteria), but papers **should be average or better in every category and should not be deficient in any category** when being considered for Distinction.

The FYC Grading Rubric was designed by a volunteer team of instructors who carefully examined a range of essays, deciding what qualities papers at different grade levels shared in common. Based on their work, we now have a common vocabulary that students and teachers can use to understand how to succeed in First-year Composition.

CHAPTER SIX

Electronic Portfolios in the First-year Composition Program

6

The First-year Composition Portfolio

Every student who takes a First-year Composition course at the University of Georgia composes an electronic portfolio over the course of the semester. The ePortfolio gives students an opportunity to revise and polish their work — even after it has been evaluated for a grade during the semester — to showcase their work in a personalized context, to reflect on their writing and their writing processes, and, finally, to "publish" their work to a broader audience.

Students develop portfolios throughout the semester using the First-year Composition program's <emma>™ writing environment, adding elements and updating and revising elements under teachers' directions and using the support available in the <emma>™ Lab in Park Hall 117. Students will also find that using feedback from their classmates in peer review sessions, both in and out of class, will make portfolio development a much more rewarding process.

The details of using <emma>™ to compose your ePortfolio will be described during Orientation sessions and during classes. In addition, individual teachers will make specific assignments for various parts of the portfolio. In broad outline, however, the essential seven components of our ePortfolios are consistent in every FYC course and are described briefly below:

Elements of the Portfolio

Biography + Image

The biography or "bio" is a short introduction to you, the author of the portfolio. Your class or teacher may specify particular information to include in your bio, but, in general, the bio should act as an author's headnote and therefore is often around 200-300 words in length.

Images on your bio page are optional, but readers like them, so you should try to include some image that is relevant. You can select a representative image (a windmill, a horse, or anything you can find on the Web — just remember to include a citation), or you can select an image of yourself. Think of it as a dust jacket image on the back of a book — how do you want to represent yourself? The goal of your Bio and Image page should be to establish a credible ethos.

> *Note: The Bio MUST be in ODT format to show properly in* <emma>™. *We strongly recommend creating it using OpenOffice. You must also check carefully to make sure that the Biography displays properly, as this will provide readers with their first impression of you as a writer.*

Reflective Introduction

The most important element in your ePortfolio, this is the introduction to the rest of the portfolio. A strong Reflective Introduction ties together all the exhibits in your portfolio; it helps you describe and reflect on your writing processes, with your exhibits providing the supporting evidence. The Reflective Introduction is also the first item evaluators will read after they open your Bio page. Your teacher may provide you with a specific prompt, unique to your section for this item, or s/he may direct you to some specific portion of the FYC program sample prompt to help you get started. In your Reflective Introduction, you will discuss how the various exhibits you have chosen for your portfolio reveal the way you have engaged with the goals of the course listed earlier in this *FYC Guide* and/or the FYC grading rubric's criteria. 500-1500 words is the average length for a Reflective Introduction.

> *Note about the Revised Essays: We recommend a thorough revision for the Revised Essays exhibits in your Portfolio — not just a quick proofreading for surface errors. Could more evidence be developed, a new perspective raised, for instance, a change in tone attempted, or a firmer line of reasoning followed?*

Revised Essay 1

This exhibit is one of the graded papers you've written for the class, revised and polished and posted to the portfolio. It should be carefully edited, error free, and completely, thoroughly, and correctly documented in MLA format.

Revised Essay 2

This exhibit is another one of the graded papers you've written for the class, revised and polished and posted to the portfolio. It should be carefully edited, error free, and completely, thoroughly, and correctly documented in MLA format.

Exhibit of Composing/Revision Process

This exhibit demonstrates your composing and revision process. Typically, students construct this document by copying and pasting the same or similar sections of a selected essay into a single document. You then add commentary to this document with the different versions, pointing out and explaining the changes you made through successive drafts. The Revision Exhibit gives you a chance to demonstrate not your best products for the semester, but the skill set that you have built up over the course.

Exhibit of Peer Review Process

One of the goals for all FYC courses states that students will "demonstrate an ability to critique the writing of themselves and others." For this exhibit, which speaks directly to that goal, you will select and post to your portfolio one of the peer reviews you have written during the semester. Choose a review you completed of one of your classmate's papers. Try to choose one that you believe was helpful and focused; you might want to ask your classmates about which ones were helpful to them. You may also copy and paste together several brief examples of peer reviews you have completed and construct a new document with inserted commentary. Explanations about the assigned peer review are often helpful here, too. As in the previous case, the Peer Review Exhibit gives you a chance to demonstrate not your best products for the semester, but the skill set that you have built up over the course.

Wild Card

This exhibit is up to you. The only limitations are that your Wild Card 1) must be an electronic file or link that "fits" in your <emma>™ portfolio; and 2) must include some of *your* writing, which may appear as captions, short descriptions, or introductory commentary. In the past, students have submitted journals, papers, photos with captions, short stories, poems, letters, song lyrics, scans of drawings with comments, news articles, podcasts, and music files. In thinking about selecting or creating a Wild Card, consider how it fits into your overall portfolio rationale and how its inclusion will impact ethos and pathos.

Special Note on Presentation and Publication of your ePortfolio

The electronic portfolio, as the capstone project that showcases your achievements and learning, is very important; it counts for about 30% of your final grade.

Furthermore, the ePortfolio is not merely a loose collection of word-processed documents, but a unified digital artifact whose parts fit together in a rational and harmonious manner. It is therefore not enough to just put your final documents in the Portfolio Prep folder. You must construct the ePortfolio using the Portfolio Tool; this is the only way that your readers can access your work. If you do not complete the ePortfolio properly, you may receive a grade of zero for this important project.

Finally, this is an *electronic* (rather than a print) portfolio that will be read online by two different readers. It is your responsibility to make sure that the front page of your ePort (biography and image) and all of the exhibits display properly without significant formatting issues.

Just as the Grading Rubric considers Presentation and Document Design as important to the rhetorical success of your essays, so too does the ePortfolio. Your portfolio therefore must meet the highest standards for presentation and document design; failure to do so will seriously hurt your grade for the ePortfolio.

Technical Note: Acceptable File Formats for ePortfolio Exhibits

Because at least two teachers must be able to read successfully your ePortfolio online and not all teachers will have available the proprietary word processing package contained on your personal computer, the FYC Program accepts only the following file formats for ePortfolio Exhibits that are primarily text documents:

- OpenOffice ODT
- PDF
- <emma>™ eDocs

While some teachers allow students to produce their work in Microsoft Word during the semester, because there can be significant formatting issues when translating Microsoft Word (.doc and .docx) documents into OpenOffice documents, we strongly recommend that you use OpenOffice, which is freely available for download from the Web, for all of your FYC work. You will be happy you chose OpenOffice when completing your ePortfolio at the end of the semester!

How Are FYC Portfolios Evaluated?

At the end of the semester, every FYC student's <emma>™ Portfolio is read by at least two FYC teachers: his or her own teacher and one other. If the scores assigned to any portfolio differ by ten or more points, a third FYC teacher also reads and scores that Portfolio. To arrive at a Final portfolio score, the two closest scores awarded are averaged. The Portfolio grade counts towards 30% of an FYC student's final course grade. (See your teacher's syllabus for more information.)

Teachers read portfolios holistically in order to evaluate them. This means that they "norm" themselves, getting a sense of what "constitutes" an A, B, C, etc. among the group of portfolios that they are reading, then judge each portfolio as a whole, assigning it a single grade. As teachers read through students' portfolios, they particularly gauge how well a student's Reflective Introduction describes the content found in the following exhibits and whether or not the student has been able to use writing to express his or her own encounter with goals and evaluative criteria of the course. In other words, expect FYC teachers to read the Reflective Introduction closely and then to examine the rest of your documents and essays to get a sense of how well they match the expectations you set up in your Introduction. Of course, teachers always look for evidence of care, originality, hard work, and excellent writing, but in the portfolio we are also interested in students' ability to write reflectively and accurately about their own writing.

In addition, teachers often use the rubric below, based on the standard FYC rubric and using the same or similar terminology, to help them get started when they are beginning to evaluate portfolios each semester. They may also point you towards this rubric to help you evaluate your own or your classmate's portfolio during a workshop.

PORTFOLIO RUBRIC

BIOGRAPHY AND IMAGE

- Is present and complete;
- Is carefully and edited, with very few errors of a grammatical, mechanical, or typographic nature.
  [CCC]______________________

- Shows clear and appropriate awareness of audience;
- Gives a coherent picture of the writer;
- Is carefully edited, with essentially no errors of a grammatical, mechanical, or typographic nature.
  [SP]______________________

- Is distinctive for its:
    - imaginative quality;
    - extraordinary and effective care in craftsmanship and presentation;
    - prose style;
    - compelling authorial voice;
    - persuasive argumentation;
    - Is carefully edited, with essentially no errors of a grammatical, mechanical, or typographic nature.

  [DIST]______________________

INTRODUCTORY REFLECTIVE ESSAY

- Is present and complete;
- Makes a clear and complete statement about the writer's ethos, development, and/or skill set that is more than an autobiographical narrative or list of exhibits (unity-thesis);
- Offers a clear rationale for the choice of exhibits and their order (unity-organization);
- Explains the role of each exhibit in the overall portfolio and in proving the thesis (evidence);
- Is carefully and edited, with very few errors of a grammatical, mechanical, or typographic nature.

  [CCC]______________________

- Offers a strong, and vivid understanding of the writer and writing (audience awareness);
- Is particularly persuasive about how exhibits contribute to the whole portfolio (coherence);
- Is carefully written and edited, with essentially no errors of a grammatical, mechanical, or typographic nature.

  [SP]______________________

- Is distinctive for its:

  imaginative quality;
  extraordinary and effective care in craftsmanship and presentation;
  prose style;
  compelling authorial voice;
  persuasive argumentation;
  Is carefully edited, with essentially no errors of a grammatical, mechanical, or typographic nature.

  [DIST]______________________

TWO REVISED CLASS ESSAYS

- Are present and complete;

- At a minimum, meet the FYC Rubric qualifications for CCC;
- Are carefully edited, with very few errors of a grammatical, mechanical, or typographic nature.

  [CCC]____

- At a minimum, meet the FYC Rubric qualifications for SP;
- Are carefully edited, with essentially no errors of a grammatical, mechanical, or typographic nature.

  [SP]____

- At a minimum, meet the FYC Rubric qualifications for a DIST or a "high" SP that shows extraordinary thoughtfulness and care;
- Are carefully edited, with essentially no errors of a grammatical, mechanical, or typographic nature.

  [DIST]____

EXHIBIT OF COMPOSING AND/OR REVISION PROCESS

- Is present and complete;
- Offers a clear and complete statement about and/or example of the composing and/or revision process (unity);
- Supports that thesis with specific examples (evidence);
- Presents the examples in a logical manner (unity-organization).

  [CCC]____

- Offers strong, and vivid examples of the writer and writing (audience awareness);
- Is particularly persuasive about how the examples support the thesis (coherence);
- Is carefully written and edited, with essentially no distracting errors of a grammatical, mechanical, or typographic nature.

  [SP]____

- Is distinctive for its:
  - imaginative quality;
  - extraordinary and effective care in craftsmanship and presentation;
  - prose style;
  - compelling authorial voice;
  - persuasive argumentation.

  [DIST]____

EXHIBIT OF PEER REVIEW PROCESS

- Is present and complete;
- Offers a clear exhibit of a peer review (unity);

- Arranges one or more examples of peer review in a logical manner (unity-organization);
- Is carefully presented so that both the original and comments are easily seen. Errors in grammar or spelling don't interfere with conveying comments (presentation & design).
  [CCC]____

- Shows a strong, and vivid understanding of the writer and commentary (audience awareness);
- Is persuasive because comments show a clear understanding and response to the work (coherence);
- Is carefully presented so that both the original and comments are easily seen. Errors in grammar or spelling don't interfere with conveying comments.
  [SP]____

- Is distinctive for its:
  - imaginative quality;
  - extraordinary and effective care in craftsmanship and presentation;
  - prose style;
  - compelling authorial voice;
  - persuasive argumentation.

  [DIST]____

WILD CARD

- Is present and complete;
- Fits into the portfolio as a whole in a logical way that is described in the introductory reflective essay;
- Is carefully written and edited, with few errors of a grammatical, mechanical, or typographic nature that distract from the purpose of the exhibit.
  [CCC]____

- Offers a strong, and vivid understanding of the writer and writing (audience awareness).
  [SP]____

- Is distinctive for its:
  - imaginative quality;
  - extraordinary and effective care in craftsmanship and presentation;
  - prose style;
  - compelling authorial voice;
  - persuasive argumentation.

  [DIST]____

CHAPTER SEVEN

Academic Honesty and Plagiarism

7

UGA Academic Honesty Policy

The University of Georgia is committed to "A Culture of Honesty." The First-year Composition Program supports this commitment and follows strictly the university's policies and procedures for dealing with possible instances of academic dishonesty. Information about "A Culture of Honesty" and the "UGA Academic Honesty Policy" and procedures can be found at the web site of the Office of the Vice President for Instruction: http://www.uga.edu/honesty/.

Plagiarism

A particular form of academic dishonesty that First-year Composition students need to understand and guard against is plagiarism. *Plagiarism* is the use of another's words or interpretations without giving credit. Plagiarism occurs when writers fail to use quotation marks to indicate exact words from a source, when they fail to paraphrase a passage completely, or when they fail to cite the source of any quotation or paraphrase.

In recent years, cutting and pasting information from the World Wide Web can lead students to commit plagiarism, particularly when they forget where the information was copied from or lose the ability to tell the difference between their own words and those copied from an electronic source. Students should also take particular care to ensure that the Wild Card exhibit for the final electronic portfolio is their own work.

To avoid plagiarism, writers should always:

1. Put quotation marks around any words from sources. When writers use an open book for writing a paper or in taking notes, or when writers take notes by cutting and pasting from an online source or website, they must be careful not to plagiarize unintentionally.
2. Paraphrase material completely; changing or rearranging a few words or the tense of a verb is not paraphrasing. Writers should read the passage to be used, close the source book or minimize the web browser, and then write in their own words what they

have read. They should then compare the paraphrase to the source; if by chance key words from the original are included, these should be changed or enclosed in quotation marks.

3. Give accurate and complete citations for all material. *The St. Martin's Handbook* gives extensive information about MLA documentation style. Writers should refer to this source when writing a paper or should consult with their instructor as to what form is required in a particular course.
4. Avoid borrowing entire arguments or approaches to a subject from another writer. In general, college papers should argue an original idea and should not be paraphrases of another writer's work. All papers that students submit must be their original work. The advantages to writers of a well-documented paper are obvious: documentation shows that writers know their subjects, and the citations give their ideas validity.

Workshop
How Not to Plagiarize

The Provost of the University of Georgia has asked FYC to conduct a program-wide workshop on plagiarism in every ENGL 1101, 1102, and 1102m class in order to support the University of Georgia's efforts to educate students on this subject. The Workshop seeks to inform students about the nature of plagiarism and about ways to avoid plagiarism in their writing.

Recognizing Plagiarism

1. Read this handout, "**How Not to Plagiarize**," for the Plagiarism Workshop.
2. Review the discussion of "**Academic Honesty and Plagiarism"** in *First-year Composition Guide, University of Georgia* (Fountainhead Press).
3. On the Web, follow the link to the University of Georgia site on Academic Honesty that is referenced in this section of *First-year Composition Guide, University of Georgia.* Review carefully the policies and procedures outlined there.
4. Review **Chapter 16** of *The St. Martin's Handbook* on "**Acknowledging Sources and Avoiding Plagiarism**."
5. On the Web, go to **"The St. Martin's Tutorial on Plagiarism.**" (See the URL for the website in Works Cited, below). When you log on as a student for the first time, you will be asked for certain information, including the email address of your instructor so that s/he can receive email reports of your quiz and exercise results. If your instructor wishes for you to provide his/her email and receive your results, s/he will tell you at this time.

Instructor email: ______________________________.

6. Read through the entire online tutorial. Review with special care the section on **"Knowing Which Sources to Acknowledge."**
7. At home / before class, work through the **"Exercise: Acknowledging Sources."** Be prepared to discuss the results of this exercise and the differences between "common knowledge" and sources that must be acknowledged at your next class meeting.
8. In-class: Discuss Homework results and then work through and discuss the Handout in this book entitled **"Citation or Plagiarism? On Using Sources Wisely**."

Acknowledging Sources

1. In "**The St. Martin's Tutorial on Plagiarism**," read the Handout "**Straight Talk about Plagiarism**."
2. Review the section on **"Taking Notes: Knowing Where Each Idea and Word Comes From"** in "**The St. Martin's Tutorial on Avoiding Plagiarism**."
3. Work through and submit the exercises on **"Recognizing Summaries," "Recognizing Paraphrases," and "Recognizing Integrated Quotations."** In your next class meeting, be prepared to discuss the results and implications of these exercises. Be prepared to ask whatever questions you may have about how to avoid plagiarism in summaries and paraphrases and about integrating quotations.

The goals of this Workshop are to support the UGA Academic Honesty Pledge—"I will be academically honest in all of my academic work and will not tolerate academic dishonesty of others"—and to help students use sources wisely in their essays.

Resources

Academic Honesty (A Culture of Honesty). Office of the Vice President for Instruction. http://www.uga.edu/honesty/.

FYC at UGA Website. http://web.english.uga.edu/newsite/fyc/home.html.

Price, Margaret. "The St. Martin's Tutorial on Avoiding Plagiarism." http://bcs.bedfordstmartins.com/plagiarismtutorial/.

"MLA Handbook Bibliographic Format for References." Research Central. http://www.libs.uga.edu/ref/mlastyle.html.

The St. Martin's Handbook Website. http://bcs.bedfordstmartins.com/smhandbook/default.asp.

Citation or Plagiarism? On Using Sources Wisely

First-year Composition, University of Georgia

Scenario #1 (completely fictional, with apologies to bears): Student A is writing an essay arguing that because bears have become a public nuisance in Missoula, Montana, a law should be passed allowing law enforcement officers to trap and release the most difficult genre of bear, the Asiatic black bear. She has found a description of this bear on the website listed below:

> ***Description:*** *The Asiatic black bear is a medium sized bear with a body length of 50 to 74 inches and weighing between 220 and 440 pounds. Females are smaller than males. They are normally blackish in color, with lighter muzzles and a distinct V-shaped patch of cream colored fur on their chest. A brown phase also occurs. The ears of an Asiatic black bear appear much larger than those of other bear species.*
> *http://www.bearden.org/asibear.html*

One body paragraph of Student A's paper reads as follows:

> This proposed law, which would allow police officers to take action against marauding bears, would be particularly helpful in stopping the rampages of the Asiatic black bears of Missoula, an easily recognizable pest on the streets of this city. The Asiatic black bear is a medium sized bear with a body length of 50 to 74 inches and weighing between 220 and 440 pounds. Females are smaller than males. They are normally blackish in color, with lighter muzzles and a distinct V-shaped patch of cream colored fur on their chest. A brown phase also occurs. The ears of an Asiatic black bear appear much larger than those of other bear species ("Asiatic Black Bear"). If the black bear were stopped, the city could get back to normal. We should take action now!

Citation or plagiarism? You make the call.

Scenario #2 (completely fictional, with apologies to bears): Student B is writing in defense of the Asian black bear, which is an endangered species in some countries. He has found the same website, which he uses as well in his paper. One body paragraph of Student B's reads as follow:

> Allowing officers to target the Asian black bear in their efforts to clean up the streets of Missoula is completely misguided because any person should be able to recognize and avoid the black bear, whose appearance is quite distinctive. The Asiatic black bear is a medium sized bear with a body length of 50 to 74 inches and weighing between 220 and 440 pounds. Females, who are smaller than males, are black and have lighter muzzles and a patch of yellow fur on their chest. Furthermore, the Asiatic black bear has larger ears than other bears ("Asiatic Black Bear").

Citation or plagiarism? You make the call.

CHAPTER EIGHT

Resources

8

Tutoring

Students who are new to the University of Georgia are often unsure about what services are available to them and where to go for help of various kinds. This section offers you places to go for help with writing, research, and personal issues.

Tutoring and Help with Writing

The university offers writers in First-year Composition a wide range of services at different locations across campus. There are three principal writing centers:

The UGA Writing Center in Park Hall

The Department of English operates the UGA Writing Center in Park Hall 66, and First-year Composition students are welcome to use its services during their FYC classes and anytime during their careers at the University of Georgia. Serving students across the campus, the Writing Center has special tutoring services for ESOL students. The Writing Center also operates a satellite center in the Science Library and holds drop-in sessions at the Miller Learning Center (MLC). For locations of these satellite centers and hours at all three locations, see the Writing Center's website at: http://writingcenter.english.uga.edu/.

Students can also get further information about services offered by the Writing Center and sign up for an appointment through the Online Appointment Signup System, which is available on the website.

Milledge Hall Tutoring Center

Located in Milledge Hall, the Division of Academic Enhancement provides appointment-based, drop-in, and online tutoring for undergraduate and graduate students across campus and disciplines. Experienced English as a Second Language specialists are available to work in person with multi-lingual students. In addition to Milledge Hall, Academic Enhancement tutoring services are available in the Miller Learning Center, in Brumby

Hall, and in the South Campus Writing Center, located in the Science Library. For more information, go to: http://www.uga.edu/dae/ and look under Services.

Aderhold Writing Center for UGA Graduate & International Students

In a cooperative venture, the Graduate School and Department of Language and Literacy Education in the College of Education have opened a writing center designed especially for UGA Graduate and International Students. For more information and to sign up for an appointment, see the flier at: http://www.coe.uga.edu/lle/awc.html.

Research

One of the biggest changes that students notice about the change between high school and university is the fact that here they are expected to do research on their own and that they are expected to know how to do quality research in a range of academic disciplines. These are big expectations, but fortunately, the UGA Libraries can help.

The UGA Libraries

Homepage: http://www.libs.uga.edu

UGA has the largest library in the state, with over 3.5 million books, thousands of periodical subscriptions, hundreds of online databases, and many librarians to help you navigate through it all. Libraries on campus include:

- ⇒ **Main Library** on North Campus: humanities, social sciences, and business;
- ⇒ **Science Library** on South Campus: science, technology, and agriculture;
- ⇒ **Miller Learning Center:** electronic library resources.

For college-level research projects and papers, your instructors will expect you to use *published scholarly resources* and *critically evaluate* any sources you take from the web. Fear not: in addition to its large book collection, the Libraries subscribe to many online databases that include articles and e-books suitable for college research. Starting at the Libraries' homepage, follow the *Books* tab to GIL, the online catalog of books in the UGA Libraries' collections. The *Articles* tab will first ask you to choose a database by subject or by name:

- ⇒ *For English 1101*, use **Academic Search Complete** for magazine and scholarly journal articles, **LexisNexis Academic** for newspaper articles and TV/radio transcripts, and **CQ Researcher Plus** for analyses of current issues.

⇒ *For English 1102/1102m*, use **JSTOR** or the **MLA International Bibliography** for literary criticism published in scholarly journals, and **Literature Resource Center** for biographies of authors.

⇒ *For any class*, use **netLibrary** for electronic books.

⇒ Ask a librarian for help choosing keywords, creating a search strategy, and for suggestions for additional databases and sources for your projects.

If you are searching from on campus (including the dorms), you will not need a password to use any of these online resources. To search from off campus, get the current password under *Password for GALILEO@UGA* on the Libraries' homepage.

Need help? Just click on *Ask a Librarian* from the Libraries' homepage, IM the reference librarians at ugalibsref or http://www.libs.uga.edu/chat, or ask at the reference desk in any of the library buildings. The research support desk at the Main and Science libraries is located on the entry floor; the research support desk at the Miller Learning Center is located in the center of the third floor. One-on-one research conferences with librarians are also available. Sign up at http://www.libs.uga.edu/ref/instruction/conform.html.

CAPS (Counseling and Psychological Services)

Everyone can use help and support at some time during his or her academic career: "Counseling and Psychiatric Services (CAPS) is dedicated to providing the best available counseling, psychiatric and psychological testing services. CAPS provides short-term individual and couples counseling, group counseling, crisis intervention, medication evaluation and monitoring, psychological testing, and makes referrals to resources on and off-campus when appropriate" (http://www.uhs.uga.edu/caps/). For more information, call 706-542-2273 or see the website from which this text was taken: http://www.uhs.uga.edu/caps/.

Whatever assistance you need, you can find it at the University of Georgia. If you are having problems—whether personal or academic—you can also ask your teacher for a referral to the proper resource.

CHAPTER NINE

What Comes Next?

9

Research into the writing process shows that the use of writing as a part of the learning process and frequency of writing are both crucial to improving and even just maintaining the writing skills and critical thinking processes that students acquire in their First-year Composition classes. What is more, employers consistently report on the importance of basic communication skills, especially in writing, for the workplace. Research has also suggested a close connection between reading and writing proficiency, and UGA students have shown that they enjoy reading and discussing books outside their formal classes. For all of these reasons, the University of Georgia encourages you to seek out other opportunities for practice in reading and writing. We would like to conclude by telling you about future opportunities to practice your literacy skills and to use writing as a powerful learning tool.

Writing Certificate Program

Beginning in 2008-2009, the University of Georgia began offering a certificate program in writing. The purpose of the Writing Certificate Program is to give undergraduate students from all colleges and majors at the University of Georgia an opportunity to develop and document their writing skills as they move from First-year Composition through the core curriculum and their academic majors en route to further education, professional training, or the workplace. Their writing skills will be developed in the context of their particular academic studies and interests and will be documented with a published electronic portfolio that presents and reflects on the students' writing projects and experiences throughout their undergraduate career. The writing done for the program will enhance students' understanding and accomplishment in their chosen field of study and will provide evidence to outside evaluators (such as admissions committees or employers) of the students' critical thinking, research, and communication skills, plus their understanding of genres and conventions of writing within their chosen discipline.

For more information about the program and its benefits, visit http://www.ctl.uga.edu/writing_certificate/.

Writing Intensive Program (WIP)

The Writing Intensive Program at the University of Georgia offers students multiple opportunities to strengthen their writing throughout their undergraduate experience by offering writing-intensive courses throughout the university in varying disciplines—from Art History to Biology to Music to Sociology, for example. A key goal of the program is to foster student writing *in the disciplines*, by helping students understand the conventions—or "ways of knowing"—of a particular discipline: how knowledge is constructed and communicated, and what rules of evidence and argumentation are practiced. To accomplish the goals of the program, each Writing Intensive Program (WIP) course is supported by a specially trained "writing coach," who works with students to improve their writing and performance in the course by providing constructive and personal feedback. The advantages of this coaching—and WIP courses, in general—are many. A compelling majority of students enrolled in these courses consistently report that their experience with the Writing Intensive Program strengthened their writing skills; built their confidence in the writing process; encouraged a deeper engagement in course reading, discussions, and assignments; taught them the writing conventions of their discipline; heightened their critical thinking skills; and prepared them for writing in other courses and future goals, such as graduate school or career-related work. **All WIP courses count toward requirements for the Writing Certificate Program**.

For more information about the program and its benefits, as well as for a list of current WIP courses, visit http:// www.wip.uga.edu.

The Major and Minor in English

The skills in writing and critical thinking that you have learned in First-year Composition will serve you well if you decide to major or minor in English. English majors learn to read, interpret, and analyze texts (novels, stories, plays, films, poems, essays, images, and other forms of cultural production) and to write with poise, brevity, and elegance. Majors can choose Areas of Emphasis for their Program of Study; areas of emphasis include Creative Writing, Multicultural Literature, Rhetoric and Composition, Humanities Computing, Studies in the Novel, Advanced Studies in English, and English Language Studies. Majors and minors can go on to careers in almost anything: teaching, publishing, law, journalism, management, human resources, medicine, grant-writing, screen-writing, technical writing, and so on. You can find more information about the English major and minor at the program website: http://www.english.uga.edu/undergrad/.

Declared English majors may also join our job club, "19 Weeks," and take ENGL 4001, Careers for English Majors. We encourage potential majors to take ENGL 4000, Introduction to the English Major, and to consult our forthcoming handbook for English majors.

Bulldog Book Club

If you want to read for pleasure, check out the Bulldog Book Club! Each meeting is a blue card event; UGA students choose the books. For more information, visit the Bulldog Book Club website at

http://fteague.myweb.uga.edu/bdbc.html

Advanced Courses in Writing

The English Department offers several upper-division courses in writing that are open to students in other majors. The Academic Enhancement Program, housed in Milledge Hall, also offers an array of writing classes for native and non-native speakers.

UNIV 1105. Improving Grammar, Usage, and Style.
3 hours.
Oasis Title: IMPROVING GRAMMAR.

> This course teaches students to master formal grammar rules and terminology, to achieve a clear, fluent writing style, and to recognize common problems of usage so that they can effectively write and edit papers for academic and professional audiences.
> **Note**: Students may enroll in this course simultaneously with ENGL 1101.

UNIV 1117. Basic Composition for Multilingual Writers.
3 hours (institutional credit).
Oasis Title: MULTILINGUAL COMP.

> This course is designed for both undergraduate and graduate students whose first language is not English. Its objectives include mastering English grammar, idioms, and sentence structure; building an academic vocabulary; and composing short academic papers. The course emphasizes problems that non-native speakers typically experience with proofreading, revision, and writing for an American audience. Assignments may be tailored to students' majors.
> **Note**: This course carries institutional credit and will not count toward graduation.

ENGL 3590. Technical Communication.
3 hours.
Oasis Title: TECH AND PROF COMM.

> This course deals with writing in the professional domains, with an emphasis on research methods, clear and accurate presentation of ideas and data, and computer-mediated communication. If you want an introduction to the role of writing in the workplace, this course would be for you.

ENGL 3600. Advanced Composition.
3 hours.
Oasis Title: ADV COMPOSITION.

Advanced Composition focuses less on professional contexts than on writing as a process, with an emphasis on the conventions of discourse situations, invention, revision, editorial skills, and document design. This course is particularly useful for students who want to practice and improve their academic writing.

ENGL 4832. Writing for the World Wide Web.
3 hours.
Oasis Title: WRITING FOR THE WEB.

This class deals with both the theory and practice of writing for the World Wide Web. Here you will learn to use the basic tools to construct web sites and be introduced to other advanced technologies useful for academic and professional writers.

ENGL 4833. Composition Theory and Pedagogy.
3 hours.
Oasis Title: COMP PEDAGOGY

This course introduces you to the history and theories of college composition teaching. With a strong practical emphasis, ENGL 4833 prepares students to work as college writing tutors or as classroom writing assistants.

CHAPTER TEN

Barnett Awards for 2009-2010

10

Barnett Awards for 2009-2010

Each year, the English Department recognizes excellent writing in English 1101, 1102, and 1102m by presenting three Barnett Awards. Named in honor of Donald E. Barnett, who directed the Freshman English Program for many years, the awards consist of cash prizes and publication of the winning essays in this pamphlet. Here are last year's winners; the essays will also be published on the First-year Composition website at: http://web.english.uga.edu/newsite/fyc/home.html.

ENGL1101
Student: Macy Marie Sirmans
Teacher: Matthew Forsythe

A Profile of Pirate Football

In the rural, Georgia town where I grew up, football exists beyond tradition. Every grandpa raised every daddy—who raises every son—to be a Pirate Football player, to lead community uproars on chilly, fall Friday nights in the giant stadium hollowed out in the hills of Hamilton. During the season, players cannot escape Jolly's Southern Restaurant without signing the football of a young admirer. Marquees of elementary schools and local businesses read "Go Pirates"

or "Keep It Up, Boys." Garages empty and windows darken at exactly 6:30 PM, giving fans an hour to find the best seat before kickoff.

I had the privilege to experience Pirate Spirit at its very best. During four of the team's most victorious years, my blonde, ribboned ponytail bounced on the sidelines as I threw plastic footballs in the stands after every touchdown, was hoisted high in the air for each kickoff, and kept a smile on my face regardless of the scoreboard. I was a Varsity Football Cheerleader. I loved the tradition of my small town, and I was a leader for its most rallying event.

For many in the town, Varsity Football games were a ritual, almost a religious experience. For me, the euphoria of a Pirate game was magical. Standing on the sidelines, I had a perfect view of the profound effects that a high school football game could have on my community. Fans, cheerleaders, band members, football players, and coaches were united and emotionally inspired as time stood still, the pursuit of victory pulsing through all of our bodies.

This is a profile of a fall Friday night in Hamilton.

The Pirate Fandom of Harriet Bass

Harriet never sat in the bleachers. She overlooked the field from the deck, an area alongside the overflowing home stands that is usually reserved for pre-game cookouts, special guests, and, of course, Harriet Bass herself. The game had not started, but Harriet was already wringing her sparkling hands anxiously.

Harriet Bass glittered. Dedicated fans described her as gaudy — borderline tacky. She was well aware of her reputation, and proud of it. Towering over the crowds at six foot four, her full-busted frame, bleached blonde hair, and bright red lipstick were unmistakable. Her fingernails were adorned with team logos—flags and Pirate heads—that coordinated with her custom-designed sweater, bedazzled with orange and blue rhinestones. The rings twinkling from eight of her fingers and one thumb, the earrings dangling to the base of her wide-set shoulders, and the massive necklace falling directly into well-defined cleavage boasted real diamonds, emeralds, and salt water pearls. Her shimmering eyelashes may have been glued to her eyelids half an hour before, but her Chanel sunglasses, Prada handbag, and bodily assets were all completely authentic, she claimed. She was a standout, a nonconformist, a self-proclaimed "Amazon Barbie Doll," and aside from her passions of tanning and shopping, Harriet was a die-hard Pirate Football fan.

For the hundredth time since arriving at the stadium, her focus darted from her pink iPhone to men wearing collared shirts with orange paw prints on their lapels. She knew the Clemson recruiters would come without warning. The coaching staff had been preparing Kevin for the surprise visit for months. She only wished that her son, blessed with her same statuesque frame and unbridled enthusiasm, was aware that his future as a Division I athlete would be determined by his performance in the night's game. Soon, number 63 would run onto the field with his closest friend and teammate, Chuck Seidel, beside him, without a glance in her direction. She would fight the urge to leap from the deck onto the sidelines and attempt to instill swiftness and passion into her son, the left guard for the offensive line.

Tonight, he couldn't afford for his best friend, number 58, to overshadow him, or cover up any of his mistakes.

Sherrie Davidson Attempts to Appear as Youthful as the Girls She Coaches

"Did you find the banner?" Holly, Captain of the Varsity Cheerleading Squad, asked the shrugging freshman.

"I know we put it in Coach Davidson's room, but I don't have the key. Do you?"

Holly and I rolled our eyes in unison. Sometimes, it was awesome to have a cheerleading coach who enjoyed gossiping, giggling, and gyrating to Lil' Wayne as much as the girls she coached. Other times, it was downright irritating.

I hastily speed-dialed her—twice. On my third try, she caught the final ring.

"Hey girl," she answered. I reminded myself not to laugh. She might be in her early 40s and answering the phone like a teenager, but she was still my cheerleading coach and AP English teacher.

"Coach Davidson, the banner is in your room. We need it for kick-off in . . . " (I glanced quickly at the scoreboard clock) "three minutes. And you have the key."

"Oh girl." She called me girl, again. "Relax. Let me finish straightening my hair, and I'll be there in a jiff. Love ya!"

Call disconnected.

Apparently, Sherrie Davidson used to be fifty pounds overweight and wore frumpy, floral dresses and thick rimmed glasses; however, I had never seen her without a full face of makeup and a tight shirt revealing a peek of a perfectly toned abdomen, nor had the rest of the cheerleading squad.

A decade before my career as a student at Central High School, Brett Buford, Sherrie's ex-husband, did more than just "peek" at another teacher. Neither of them left CHS after their divorce. Sherrie continued to teach English and Sociology and coach the cheerleading squad. Matt was still the Driver's Education Teacher and the tight-end coach. Post-divorce, nose job, butt lift, breast augmentation, and braces, Sherrie Davidson transformed into a mid-life bombshell, which was why before every football game, instead of supervising and coaching the Varsity cheerleading squad, Sherrie would drive her re-furbished 1981 Mustang (with the top down) to her house, squeeze into a pair of hip-hugging jeans, orange tank top, and high heels, and make it back to campus in time to parade down the bleacher steps as the coaches filed onto the sidelines.

As players made their way onto the field, Holly and I shot each other anxious looks. Coach Davidson had better make it back to Pirate Stadium before kickoff.

Raymond Banks Prepares for Personal Victory

I'd known Raymond since kindergarten. His first day of school, he staggered into the classroom.

"What's wrong with your legs?" we all asked.

Raymond shrugged his shoulders. "Always been like this," he answered. His head fell forward toward the ground, and he sighed. "Always will be like this."

Raymond Banks suffered from severe curvatures of the bones in his legs, making it nearly impossible for him to walk. Growing up, walking wasn't Raymond's only struggle. A learning disability isolated him from his classmates, and his deformity made him an object of ridicule during more than one recess in elementary school. Raymond never had the potential to play sports or compete in academic competitions. He wasn't able to hold a job and had very few friends. Until his teenage years, Raymond excelled at very little. Then, he discovered the saxophone.

When Raymond joined Central's Marching Pirates, he finally met people who appreciated him for the gifts he possessed—compassion and perseverance. Motivated by the band director and his peers, Raymond learned to play the saxophone. Throughout high school, Raymond could almost always be seen inside the band room practicing, or waiting outside the band room for an opportunity to practice. However, despite his hard work and obvious talent, the bones in Raymond's legs prevented him from ever marching with his fellow band members during a football game.

It was his senior year, and the first successful surgery had been performed on Raymond the summer before. After extensive physical therapy, he was finally able to stand upright and walk without a cane. Maybe tonight, finally tonight, Raymond Banks would perform with the Marching Pirates during halftime.

Chuck Seidel Has the Heart of a Pirate Athlete

It was fourth down, with seven yards to go, and the ball rested on the opponent's twelve yard line. After a lengthy timeout, the Pirates decided to go for it—to attempt to score a touchdown, or at least make it to first and goal. Fifteen hundred orange and blue fans quieted in the stadium bleachers, allowing a moment of peace for the offense's concentration.

Necks craned in the direction of the opponent's end zone after the snap. We held our breath as the quarterback prepared for flawless execution. A lone receiver waited to make the catch. Cheers began to erupt when—the quarterback was sacked.

The offensive line walked sluggishly from the damp field, jerking off their helmets. Offensive line coach Matt Washington waited for them beside a sweat-soaked metal bench.

"Have a seat, boys!" Washington yelled over the roar of the band, cheerleaders, and crowd.

He looked into the eyes of each of the young men before him—players he had coached since the beginning of their varsity careers. Washington knew the boys' families and understood their weaknesses and most noteworthy accomplishments. Spending multiple seasons together on the CHS practice field and Pirate Stadium sidelines had given the offensive line and their coach an appreciated intimacy. Washington's eyes fell on the player he most admired and trusted—Chuck Seidel.

"Chuck." Washington's face ventured close to his. "What's going on out there?"

Looking into the eyes of the coach he respected and the friend he adored, Chuck Seidel had never been more trusting, or more certain. When the five offensive linemen took the field, Chuck was aware of not only his own movements, but also those of his comrades beside him. He could instantly pinpoint hitches in the line's formation and execution, and he was almost as swift as Washington in contriving alternate tactics for success.

"It's the interior of the line," Chuck responded. Hesitant to continue, he glanced at his best friend and fellow offensive lineman, Kevin Bass. "I think the opposing defensive guard may be giving Kevin a few problems."

Kevin Bass had four inches and thirty pounds on Chuck, but Chuck was a swift thinker and incredible talent. Despite Kevin's many athletic strengths, he eagerly accepted criticism and suggestions from his insightful friend. The two had been best friends since they'd played football together as kids. Chuck was always the center, and Kevin was always his "wingman" as left guard. Together, they had ventured from tiny football fields at the Hamilton Recreation Department to the bright lights of Pirate Stadium. They had spent multiple weekends sharing beer and ambition in the serenity of Kevin's back yard, and had spent lazy summers together at Chuck's lake property. The two did not have to speak to know what each other was thinking. Chuck knew that Kevin often tired of long two-a-days in the heat of summertime, and the pressure to succeed often overwhelmed him. Kevin, however, knew that Chuck was ceaselessly motivated and focused, during both daily practices and Friday's games.

"I know I could succeed at anything in life, anything!" Kevin had told Chuck a few months earlier. "If I only had half the heart you have for Pirate Football."

Chuck loved football. During the fall, he lived and breathed it. He was fueled by game-day moments — like the sensation of cold air hitting his chest through his shoulder pads as he walked with his teammates towards the stadium crowded with boisterous fans. The entire coaching staff respected Chuck. He watched game film in his spare time, always attempting to perfect his already faultless snaps. He had the soul and spirit of a talented Pirate athlete. He had earned the coveted Heart of a Pirate and Offensive Line awards two years in a row. He was an invaluable component to CHS victories.

Chuck dreamed of playing football for a promising D-I university. But just as he was aware of his many strengths, Chuck knew that his height, five feet and ten inches, would hold him back in the collegiate arena. Recruiters had agreed with the CHS coaches. Seidel was one of the most skilled centers in the state of Georgia. If only these same recruiters could overlook the simple flaw in his perfection—his height.

Considering Chuck's analysis of the line's mishaps, Matt Washington retrieved the dry-erase board and tiny black marker reserved for quick offensive alterations. His bald head reflected the vivid stadium lights. Washington and Chuck collaborated, creating a new blocking scheme better suiting the force of the offensive line.

"Can you guys handle this?" Chuck asked his teammates.

Four heads nodded in unison.

Chuck glanced at Kevin. "You cool with it?"

Kevin chuckled. "Damn right I am. Just do what you do best."

The offensive line took the field once again. This time, Chuck was face to face with the monstrous left tackle. The most intimidating player from the opposing team would battle against Chuck Seidel's adroit perception. Earlier, a casual blunder from Kevin Bass had ended with a sack. With Chuck Seidel in charge, the play resulted in a touchdown.

After a competitive and tense Friday night, Hamilton was defeated by a mere field goal in the final seconds of the fourth quarter. Players staggered off the field, beaten, stinking, and covered in grass, but not conquered. I walked briskly from the sacred confines of Pirate Stadium, just in time to hear the last of the boys' cleats file into the locker room for showers, pinches of tobacco, and a few last moments in the company of teammates and buddies. Yet despite a brutal loss, the post-game atmosphere was not full of defeat and remorse. Pirate Football not only unites a variety of people, but it also inspires a broad array of emotions.

For Kevin Bass, the post-game atmosphere was one of achievement. He looked away from his intense conversation with the Clemson recruiters just long enough for me to offer him a brief wink and a thumbs up. For Kevin, there would be four more years.

For Sherrie Davidson, the atmosphere was one of hopefulness. "Better luck next week," she said with a sigh, as I gave her a quick, one-armed hug. Although she alluded to the fate of the game, she glared longingly in the direction of Coach Buford, engaged in conversation with a vibrant young teacher from the science department. For Sherrie, there would be another opportunity to snag his eye on Monday morning.

For Raymond Banks, the post-game atmosphere was one of celebration. I gave him a congratulatory pat on the back as I passed him. His hands were still wrapped around his beloved saxophone as he mentally relived his moments of marching on the field during halftime, barely an hour earlier. For Raymond, there would be the contentment of finally excelling.

For Harriet Bass, the atmosphere was one of relief. From across the crowd gathered outside of the locker room, I blew her a kiss. She caught it, giggled, and pretended to stuff it into her orange Prada handbag. For Harriet Bass, there would be another opportunity for Pirate spirit.

And for Chuck Seidel, the post-game atmosphere was ironic. He finally ambled out of the locker room, forlorn without 63 by his side. I collided with him in the same warm hug and savory kiss he'd received from me after every high school football game. Hand in hand, we slowly made our way to the serenity of his black pickup truck — through the proud handshakes from the coaching staff and showers of high-fives from his teammates.

For Chuck, there wouldn't be four more years. Only a few Friday nights under the lights of our local stadium remained. Soon, the cuts on his knuckles, mementos of Friday night battles, would turn to scars. Chuck Seidel was inches short of his collegiate dreams as a Division I athlete. Yet, as he wrapped his arms around my shoulders and glanced back at what would become the most exciting and intense part of his past, we both knew that the fans, emotions, and consequences of Pirate Football barely mattered. For Chuck, there would always be love and encouragement. Despite the opinions of high school football coaches or D-I college recruiters, he knew he would always be ranked my number one.

I'm now a freshman at UGA—reputed in Hamilton to be "The Harvard of the South." I am a recent sorority girl, and my blonde ponytail now bounces on the catwalk they call a campus. Along with the the rest of my 2009 Freshman Class with the privilege to reside in Athens, I am the envy of many. So why, when I behold that sunken Hamilton stadium, which suddenly isn't so giant in comparison to Sanford Stadium, does my heart yearn for the tranquility of my high school years? Why will I always feel that I belong on the sidelines of Pirate Stadium, even as the next lineup of girls replaces me?

As precious as my days as a high school cheerleader were, they are not my glory days. Over time, bigger and better accomplishments will replace sideline memories, and my years as a Pirate will inspire nothing more than a fleeting smile. Yet there will never be a time when I will not drive past my high school and remember the sound of the loudspeaker announcing a winning score, the smell of freshly cut grass and sweaty athletes, and the lights that illuminated the Friday night sky.

The names across the backs of the CHS jerseys are different now. Seats are filled with some new Pirate supporters, but most of the fans are the same. Football and cheerleading coaches move up and on, and marching musicians, cheerleaders, and football players graduate and continue to their next opportunity. Despite the changing times, the essentials of Pirate Football will not alter much from year to year. Tobacco-chewing farmers and affluent community businessmen will still sit together on stadium bleachers. The aroma of boiled peanuts and hot chocolate will still drift intoxicatingly from the concession stand. Students will still paint their bodies orange and blue, and cheer half-naked in freezing weather. And little boys, footballs in their arms, will still view the entirety of a football game from a grassy patch overlooking the field, mimicking the movements and aggression of the players down below, preparing for the fall Friday nights in Pirate Stadium when they will carry on a heartfelt community tradition.

---

* Names and football numbers throughout the course of the essay have been changed.

ENGL1101
Student: John Mays
Instructor: Nathan Camp

"Maharaj Cotton"
How the Death of "King Cotton" Led to Increased British Interests in India

In the 1830s, the Southeastern states were developing as a new economic power. The new growth was due to one crop—cotton. By 1860, nearly sixty percent of the total United States export was cotton. This cash crop pushed the young nation onto the world economic stage. In 1861, the nascent Confederacy was totally dependent on this "King" of the economy, and it played a major role in the Confederacy's downfall. As the American War Between the States dragged on and the Union blockade on Confederate ports remained in place, cotton exports decreased from a mighty river to a trickle. British textile mills, dependent on this supply, ground to a halt, and an alternative source of cotton had to be found. The eyes of a desperate Britain fell on India, and as "King Cotton" destroyed one country, it gave birth to another. Though the sphere of influence of cotton during the War Between the States is normally restricted to the United States, the deficit of southern cotton caused an increased British interest in the governing and development of India as a cotton producer.

Prior to the invention of the cotton gin in 1794, large-scale production of long-staple cotton in the South was largely impractical. Long-staple cottons are known and named for their long fibers and high quality, and these varieties were desired by textile mills in Britain because they could be made into high-quality cloth. After the invention of the cotton gin, southern production rose dramatically from just a few hundred bales in the early 1800s to over five million bales in 1860 (Pope). During the same period, India was somewhat restricted in its development because England was at war with France, and the French attacked vessels laden with Indian cotton in an attempt to disrupt the British economy. Chapman notes that during this time America remained neutral, and cotton trade was allowed to flourish (63). During a time when India could have been developing, it was being repressed, and when international conditions allowed trade to resume, British textile mills had already become dependent on American cotton.

British textile mills in the Manchester-Lancashire area of England during the Antebellum years were the world's leading consumers of cotton. In *The History of the Cotton Famine*, Arnold states that the "required food" of the Manchester area textile mills was 1,051,623,380 pounds of cotton. To satisfy this hunger, Britain imported 1,390,938,752 pounds of cotton (37). Of that, America sent over 1,115,890,608 pounds (38). Through simple calculation, one can derive that American cotton constituted eighty percent of British cotton imports. This over-dependence on one source of cotton did not alarm many in position to remedy the problem, and the only real actions taken to diversify cotton sources were a handful of commissions to study India by the Manchester Chamber of Commerce (Silver 60). The government purposefully stayed out of attempts to develop India at this time and refused to finance official expeditions to India (64). Logan writes that in an eerie moment of prescience, a newspaper from Bolton, England raised the question of how an American civil war would "suddenly [choke] the sources of that enormous . . . supply" (qtd. in Logan 472). The newspaper writer was surely not at all surprised when just that happened a few years later.

The attack on Fort Sumter in April 1861 signaled the beginning of Britain's cotton problem. However, many Britons were in disbelief at the seriousness of the coming conflict, and Arnold writes, "We persisted in believing that this interchange . . . was nothing more than a game of brag" (40). Once the Union enacted the Anaconda Plan and Union ships blockaded southern ports, the export of cotton was almost non-existent. Confederate foreign policy hinged on the dependence of Britain on southern cotton, and an effort was made to force Britain to break the blockade to save their own cotton industry, but this was to no avail. The United Kingdom declared themselves to be neutral and took the risk of their own ruin into their own hands. As a result, the blockade remained in place and continued to restrict trade with the Confederacy. On top of the fact that very little cotton was getting out of the Confederacy, William T. Sherman led his army on a destructive mission through some of the most cotton-rich areas of Georgia and South Carolina. The destruction of this fertile farmland further subtracted from the ability of the South to provide for the massive needs of the British textile industry. In the years between the 1860 and 1870 censuses, cotton production of the South decreased from 5,331,439 bales (2,132,575,600 pounds) to 3,008,848 bales (1,203,539,200 pounds) (Pope). It should be noted that even in 1870, the South could have supplied a large portion of England's demand, but there was also a demand in New England that had to be met. During the Reconstruction years, domestic needs took precedence over foreign ones. Both the scarcity of cotton during the War Between the States and the deficit of production after the war led to a period known in England as the "Cotton Famine."

The Cotton Famine had been expected by few and affected many. About 440,000 people worked in the textile mills of the Manchester-Lancashire area, and after the cotton supply from the South was cut off, nearly half a million workers and family members were receiving help for their unemployment (Arnold 35; 44). The dangerous dependence on a single supply of cotton could not be ignored any longer. The "game of brag" had become a full-fledged war, and the British cotton industry was caught in the middle. Even after the War Between the States, cotton prices were inflated from $35.98/bale to $75.45/bale. This means that the total costs of British imports would have doubled from $100,374,360.19 to $210,484,865.93. Aside from the unavailability of southern cotton, Britain had to now consider the economy of continuing to import from the South.

Spurred on by the scarcity of southern cotton during the War Between the States, the British Empire looked to its various possessions and territories overseas, including India, for a new source of cotton. The East India Company had been experimenting with various breeds of cotton since 1811 and found a few that produced bolls of both the quality and quantity of American varieties (Silver 95). When the British government took control of India in 1858, the East India Company had mismanaged the cotton industry terribly. The Company had terrible practices for storing the cotton, including burying it, which irreversibly contaminated the product. Lower-quality cotton was mixed into the cotton of marketable quality. This mixing caused a decrease in the price of the cotton and created problems at the mills in Britain (30). The *ryots*, small-scale peasant farmers, were only concerned with getting fast payment from the Company and not with the quality of their product (33). In 1861, when the situation became desperate, the government, now in control of India, issued two proclamations with the intention of increasing both the quantity and the quality of cotton produced in India. The first proclamation dictated that each region of India should gather information about how to better the production of cotton in their region. The second offered a reward of ten thousand *rupees* to the plantation in each region that produced both the highest quality and highest quantity cotton (Logan 474-75). Because of this new monetary incentive, the second proclamation seems the most likely source for the *ryots*' interest in producing good-quality, high-quantity cotton. Because of the lack of cotton from the South in 1861, textile mills were buying cotton at much higher prices when they could get it. This led to more production simply because of the promise of more money (475). The combination of the proclamations and the rise in prices paid off for British textile companies. In 1862, Britain imported 1,133,000 bales (453,200,000) of cotton and India contributed 1,069,000 bales (427,600,000) (476). Though British importation was still severely depressed from the 1,390,938,752 pounds that they had imported in 1860, they had found a new source of cotton that could be developed into a successful replacement for the deficit in southern cotton production.

Cotton cultivation continued to expand in India throughout the War Between the States to provide for the continual need of the textile mills and to help the economy of the Manchester-Lancashire area to recover. Production rose from 1,069,000 bales (427,600,000) in 1861 to 1,398,000 bales (559,200,000 pounds) in 1864 (Logan 476). This increase in production could not yet replace the billion pounds of cotton that the South exported to Britain every year, but it was the first step.

The legacy of cotton development in India lasts to this day. As of 2009, India was second in both overall production and exports of cotton (*Rankings*). The influences of cotton in India are not just agricultural. The rise in cotton production brought in much needed outside capital. Government intervention prevented the East India Company from destroying the country in its quest for wealth. Indian infrastructure had to be developed to move cotton from the interior to the sea. This meant the construction of roads and railroads that are still in use today (Logan 474). The *ryots* became more middle-class and less lower-class. They were able to purchase many items that were previously too expensive for them to afford (Logan 478). Also, the mercantile nature of the British Empire meant that all cotton produced in India had to be sent to Britain, and then Indians had to buy the products of British mills. Mohandas Gandhi protested this policy by spinning his own yarn and weaving his own cloth, which was illegal at the time. In a way, the increased cotton production in India led to the Indian Revolution.

Though 1860 was a long time ago, the events of that time had a great and far-reaching impact. The bond of the United States was put to the test. Lincoln issued the Emancipation Proclamation. India took its first steps on its path to economic power. The War Between the States played a much larger role on the world stage than some believe. The United States' single biggest export was the United Kingdom's single biggest import. As "King Cotton" died in the West, "Maharaja Cotton" was born in the East. Some may say, "Britain did not just get cotton out of India," and they are right, but why did Britain go to India in the first place? The need for cotton led Britain to India and created the British Empire as it was known for a hundred years. The need for cotton took India from being a group of warring principalities to becoming a united country. The need for cotton created India as it is today.

Works Cited

Arnold, Arthur. *The History of the Cotton Famine: From the Fall of Sumter to the Passing of the Public Works Act*. London: Saunders, Otley, and Co., 1864. 21 Jan. 2008. Web. The Internet Archive. PDF. 23 Oct. 2009.

Chapman, John. *The Cotton and Commerce of India, Considered in Relation to the Interests of Great Britain*. London: John Chapman, 1851. The Internet archive. n.d. Web. 2 Nov. 2009.

Logan, Frenise A. "India—Britain's Substitute for American Cotton, 1861-1865." *The Journal of Southern History* 24.4 (1958): 472-80. JSTOR. Web. 2 Nov. 2009.

Pope, John W. R. "Cotton Production Facts." Editorial. *New York Times*. 6 July 1883: 6. Web. 2 Nov. 2009.

Rankings. National Cotton Council of America. n.d. Web. 2 Nov. 2009.

Silver, Arthur W. *Manchester Men and Indian Cotton, 1847-1872*. Manchester: Manchester University Press, 1966. Google Books. n.d. Web. 26 Oct. 2009.

Works Consulted

Habib, Irfan. "Colonialization of the Indian Economy, 1757-1900." *Social Science* 3.8 (1975): 23-53. JSTOR. Web. 2 Nov. 2009.

"Value, U.S. Exports, Imports." Rand McNally and Company. 1897. Chart. *David Rumsey Map Collection*. David Rumsey Map Collection. Web. 2 Nov. 2009.

ENGL1101
Student: Olivia Swint
Teacher: Caroline Bartunek

Rise Against: Speaking Out Against War

The punk rock band, Rise Against, was born in Chicago, Illinois in 1999. Their first album, *The Unraveling*, was released in 2001 (*Keep Music Alive*). The band has since produced four albums (*Rise Against: Official Site*). Current band members, Tim McIlrath performing vocals, Joe Principe at bass guitar and vocals, Brandon Barnes on drums, and Zach Blair on lead guitar, follow a liberal, political ideology, according to a profile by Ryan Cooper. They have been a part of Punk Voter, and they endorse PETA, People for the Ethical Treatment of Animals, which follows the same political ideologies (Cooper). Many of their songs are about standing up to the injustices occurring in the world. Their latest album, *Appeal to Reason*, tackles issues like corporate America, the declining environment, and the war in Iraq. Lead singer, Tim McIlrath, explains that the members of Rise Against want to use their punk rock music as "a vehicle for change and awareness" ("An Interview"). Rise Against has successfully employed its music and music videos as tools to raise awareness about issues in contemporary society, specifically instances of torture that have taken place during the war in Iraq.

The music video for "Hero of War," a song from their latest album, *Appeal to Reason*, embodies a spirit of enlightenment, revealing to the audience the emotional effects of war on a soldier who has first-hand experience on the battlefield. "Hero of War" was written to "remind people of these events while they're happening," says McIlrath, and he uses Abu Ghraib, a prison in Iraq, as an example of one of "these events" ("Interview: Rise Against"). The music video opens with a shot of McIlrath playing an acoustic guitar, sitting in a plastic chair against the backdrop of a playground. The playground is deserted, empty of youth; there are no children laughing, playing, or running around. The melancholy setting portrays the loss of innocence by a young man forced to grow up fast. The camera returns to this scene several times throughout the video to emphasize that war takes away youthfulness. The shots then begin to alternate amongst several scenes, each portraying the same man as a soldier with a young woman and through night-vision lenses. As the main character of the video, the young man represents the tale of a man brave enough to leave his home and family because of his love for his country. Soldiers on patrol represent the usual day-to-day life when first arriving in the war, doing basic duties like keeping guard. The soldier becomes more involved in combat, which leads to scenes of him and another soldier torturing a prisoner-of-war by waterboarding. While waterboarding is not specifically mentioned in the song, the scene overlaps the verse, "They took off his clothes, they pissed in his hands / I told them to stop, but then I joined in / We beat him with guns and batons / Not just once, but again and again." The verse implies that the "him" in these lyrics and the man being tortured in the video represents the Iraqi detainees who suffered at the hands of a few American soldiers at Abu Ghraib, spotlighting these events as McIlrath intended.

Before he left for the war, the young soldier was full of love and happiness. He had to leave his sweetheart behind. He painfully, but proudly explained that he had a duty to fight for his country, and he promised to return to her. As he transitions into the military, the soldier clings to his sweetheart's photograph. The young woman represents the happiness and innocence of his former life and provides hope of one day returning to normalcy. The war begins to wear on the soldier, and he eventually finds himself consumed and beaten by temptation to partake in the torture of the prisoner.

When the young man is shown through night-vision lenses, he throws his body around and yanks at his hair, and his face is contorted in anguish. He sobs and beats his fists against the mirror and floor. His memory flashes back prior to the war, to a time that was happy for him. He has returned home, but he is in a deep depression. The agony caused by the torture he witnessed and administered has put him into darkness. At the end of the video, he emerges from this horrible darkness with white paint smeared across his face. His ghostly image is an externalization of the deadness he feels inside, the result of the internal conflict with which he has been struggling.

The story depicted in the music video is based on events that occurred at Abu Ghraib. According to Seymour Hersh, before it became a United States Military prison, Abu Ghraib was under the control of Saddam Hussein and was characterized by "torture, weekly executions, and vile living conditions." The prison received a desperately needed upgrade, including bathrooms, a medical center, and a good overall cleaning in order to accommodate prisoners-of-war humanely. Unfortunately, these improvements did not keep prisoners from illegal abuses. Six suspects, all members of the United States Army, faced charges including conspiracy, cruelty toward prisoners, maltreatment, assault, and indecent acts. During the hearing in the case of Staff Sargeant Ivan L. Frederick II, witnesses told of instances where prisoners were seen being forced to masturbate one another and left naked in isolation cells without water, a toilet, or ventilation for several days. Sargeant Frederick claimed that he had questioned the maltreatment of prisoners but was told by higher powers not to worry about it. One man who had seen prisoners thrown into a pile by another Army soldier when he delivered them to the prison testified that he had reported the action to his superiors assuming that they would take care of the problem (Hersh).

Military Intelligence implied that these abuses were acceptable by congratulating the suspects for a good job of loosening up prisoners for interrogation by unethical methods such as depriving them of sleep. They needed information from the detainees and had no qualms about forcing them to perform acts that, in essence, stripped them of their humanity. General Janis Karpinski, who was placed in charge of Abu Ghraib, had a difficult time finding fault with the situation. When graphic photographs were released and horrified the public, society finally realized that a change was necessary (Hersh). The outcry against them motivated the reform of military prison practices and demanded oversight to prevent these events from occurring again.

The underlying theme of men returning home who have been tortured by their experiences is present in the music video. According to Brett Schwartz, "Twenty percent of [soldiers who have served in Iraq or Afghanistan] are experiencing Post Traumatic Stress Disorder (PTSD) and/or depression from the exposure to combat" (8). In November 2007, it was reported that every week, 120 veterans committed suicide, resulting in 6,256 veteran suicides in 2005. "Veterans between the ages of twenty and twenty-four were the demographic most likely to commit suicide," a rate three times greater than the rate of civilian suicides in the same age category (B. Schwartz 8). Rise Against has been influenced to spread awareness about these alarming statistics and the severe mental effects that war has on soldiers. Tim McIlrath takes a moment before live performances of "Hero of War" to share these facts with the audience. Instead of just reminding people about what happened in Abu Ghraib, he wants people to know that there are men and women who have put their lives at stake for this country, but have come home scarred by their experiences. These soldiers are waging an internal war with PTSD and the constant reminders of the horrors of these experiences.

Despite the efforts to raise awareness, Rise Against has been accused of not supporting the men and women of the military. The band has always been vocally opposed to the war, but they have never been against the troops fighting in the war. In early October 2009, Florida radio station WPBZ (Buzz 103.1) tried to convince its listeners that Rise Against was actually against all things military. In their online blog, the band clarified that Buzz's animosity came after Rise Against backed out of performing in the station's annual music festival. This decision was made after the band found out that the show was going to be sponsored by the United States Army's Recruitment Department. Since the band has been openly opposed to some of the tactics used by the department to recruit new members, they felt that it would be hypocritical to hold a performance supporting ideals with which they did not agree. Rise Against has performed at multiple military bases for the troops and has allowed troops and their families to attend other performances for free as a show of their support for the soldiers (L. Schwartz).

The content of Rise Against's music has been affected by the problematic events of modern society. The war in Iraq is one of the most significant of these events. This war is surrounded by controversy, and the band wants to bring this issue to their audience's attention. The band is reaching out to a current generation of listeners who are young and feel disenfranchised. They want their listeners to be informed about what is happening in the world and then encourage them to stand up and speak out if they are concerned with all of the problems. Rise Against's songs recommend action be taken while also preserving some of the cultural feelings towards issues, so that future generations may look back and understand what was going on in society during that time.

Works Cited

Cooper, Ryan. "Rise Against Profile—A Brief Biography of Rise Against." *About.com: Punk Music*. The New York Times Company. Web. 20 Oct. 2009. <http://punkmusic.about.com/od/riseagainst/p/Rise Against.htm>.

Hero of War. Dir. Meiert Avis, Chris LeDoux, and Jason Lehel. Prod. Jeremy Alter and Nicole Ehrlich. Perf. Rise Against. YouTube, LLC, 21 May 2009. Web. 20 Oct. 2009. <http://www.youtube.com/watch?v=PpnWgCVfAxw>.

Hersh, Seymour M. "Torture at Abu Ghraib." *The New Yorker*. 10 May 2004. Web. 20 Oct. 2009. <http://www.newyorker.com/archive/2004/05/10/040510fa_fact>.

"Interview: Rise Against." Interview. *ARTIST* direct. ARTIST direct INC, 14 Dec. 2008. Web. 20 Oct. 2009. <http://www.artistdirect.com/entertainment-news/article/interview-rise-against/4894898>.

"An Interview With Tim McIlrath of Rise Against — June, 2006." Interview by Ryan Cooper. *About.com: Punk Music*. The New York Times Company, June 2006. Web. 5 Oct. 2009.

Rise Against. "Hero of War." *Appeal to Reason*. Geffen, 2008. CD.

"Rise Against." Keep Music Alive. Vbulletin, 2 Feb. 2008. Web. 4 Oct. 2009. <http://www.keepmusicalive.com/featured-artist-rise-against-t4191.html>.

Rise Against: Official Site. DGC Records. Web. 5 Oct. 2009. <http://www.riseagainst.com>.

Schwartz, Brett. "A Different Kind of Enemy: American Soldiers Face Mental Health Challenges After Returning Home." *The Defense Monitor*, Jul./Aug. 2008 37.4 (2008): 8-9. *Academic Search Complete*. Web. 26 Oct. 2009. <http://web.ebscohost.com/ehost/pdf?vid-3&hid=9&sid=ce2e9866-42d7-4a85-a659-177d-949967e%40sessionmgr4>.

Schwartz, Lorraine. "Chicago Punk Rockers Rise Against vs. the U.S. Army? Not." *Examiner.com*. Clarity Digital Group, LLC, 2 Oct 2009. Web. 5 Oct. 2009. <http://www.examiner.com/x-7025-NY-Concert-Examiner~2009m10d2-Chicago-punk-rockers-Rise-Against-vs-The-US-Army-Not>.

ENGL1102
Student: Darcy Lenz
Instructor: Lisa Reeves

Father Knows Best

Picture a typical businessman sauntering through the white picket fence of his pristine home following a long, yet thoroughly satisfying day at the office. The odors of an alluring dinner prepared by his devoted wife greet him while two all-American youngsters race to embrace their dear ol'dad. As this affectionate, fictitious family sits down for a pleasant meal, they uphold the hollow precedent that countless individuals fail to achieve. Despite the family portrait the Cleavers may faithfully promise from the television screen, a "perfect" family simply does not and cannot exist. However, the reality of the matter does not prevent many from diligently defending the concept. Such delusional perceptions generally result in a painful sense of shortcoming for family members drowning in the pressures of idealism, inevitably resulting in the family unit's gradual deterioration. The Lomans in Arthur Miller's *Death of a Salesman* and the Hoover family in the movie *Little Miss Sunshine* serve as two pertinent examples of this ironically unfortunate phenomenon. Driven by the patriarchal figures' denial and general disdain for those "not-liked" or "losers," both families illustrate the image of dysfunction as the various family members desperately attempt to uncover some level of honesty within their households.

In the Loman home, anything short of perfection is absolutely intolerable . . . at least in theory. The head of the family, Willy Loman, centers all family activity around the maintenance of a flawless family image. Consequently, he utterly refuses to acknowledge the existence of any negative attributes that may counter his dream, thus sacrificing his relatives' actual needs. For a number of years, Willy's facade works quite well. He is a seemingly successful salesman with two strapping sons "built like Adonises" and a submissive wife who loyally supports her husband's warped visions (Miller 1081). After all, he is the head of the household; thus, his actions and beliefs greatly manipulate the thoughts and actions of his wife and children, providing him with a false sense of security. In psychological terms, such behavior is known as "the recursive nature of living systems . . . When one person in the system acts, every other person is influenced, which again affects the person who initially acted" (Conoley 2). All the same, the Loman lifestyle is far from ideal. Regardless of his owning appliances with "the biggest ads" and fathering a high school celebrity, Willy's obsession with an immaculate family image eventually becomes the destructive force responsible for his family troubles and overall mental instability (Miller 1082). In fact, even his sons' adolescent glory days reveal that Willy's insecurities are laying a foundation for future family trauma. As he ignores his eldest son completely, the father essentially worships Biff and encourages the lad's miscreant behaviors, such as cheating, stealing, and being "too rough with the girls" (Miller 1084).

Beyond instilling relatively immoral values into his children in his attempt to make certain they are "well liked," Willy incessantly disrespects the one person who faithfully nurtures him and views him as "the handsomest man in the world," his wife Linda (Miller 1080, 1083). At home Willy frequently releases frustration upon his wife, yelling at her for hardly notable offenses such as "interrupting," mending her stockings, or "contradict[ing]" his cheese preferences (Miller 1096, 1073). Of course, while traveling, the combination of being "so lonely" and fearing he "won't make a living for [Linda]" compels Willy to repetitively cheat on his "pal" of a wife (Miller 1083). Secretly tainting his marriage with deceit is but a single example of Willy's American dream family existing solely within the bounds of his mind, rather than in reality. Despite the escalating internal problems, Willy is determined to convince himself, along with the rest of his family and friends, that "there's nothing the matter" with the Lomans (Miller 1084). Unfortunately, one cannot force a family into a frame of perfection through reputation alone, a fact that torments each member of the family from the moment Biff fails high school algebra.

Much like the Lomans, the Hoover family is wrought with conflict as a result of the attempt to fit within the father's perfect mold. Also a salesman, Richard Hoover relentlessly pushes his "Nine Steps to Success" plan upon his family, as well as anyone else who will listen. Like Willy, Richard fails in selling his product to customers, but severely traumatizes his family with his dogged ideals of success. However, the Hoovers as a whole, in contrast with the Loman family, are considerably less secretive about their personal dysfunction. The overly competitive Richard has fathered two children: a depressed son and a chunky, spunky, pageant-crazed daughter, Olive. Additionally, the family hosts a suicidal, homosexual uncle and a porn/drug-addicted grandfather. Paralleling Linda Loman, the desperate Hoover mother frantically tries to hold her family together, as far from picture perfect as they may be. Nonetheless, these openly eccentric characters provide a similar example of the emotional struggles the Lomans fight to keep beneath the surface. The movie's plot focuses on a family road trip, encouraged by Mr. Hoover's thirst for victory, to a beauty pageant so that young Olive can compete for the title of "Little Miss Sunshine." The numerous trials which the Hoovers face along the way, such as the grandfather's death, constant transportation trouble, and numerous psychological "meltdown[s]," provide a "look at the ceaseless and futile battle to maintain one's footing on a social treadmill" (Laurier). This relentless combat against social expectations effectively proves the standard of a faultless family to be undeniably unattainable. As Richard refuses to accept his family and himself in their state of imperfection, the tensions between relatives grow through the "recklessly blind and egotistical quest" (Laurier).

As with any object withstanding immense pressure, a family, too, must ultimately fold under mounting weight; and in the case of the Lomans, the members walk away with a number of lasting psychological scars. Their denial, rather than the actual family discrepancies, ultimately disbands the family. The paramount dilemma in fostering a family living in pure denial is that at least one member will more than likely stumble upon some form of enlightenment, which predictably makes for chaos amongst the remaining family members. Such an epiphany strikes Biff as he discovers his father's infidelity. The boy's sense of perception is drastically shaken as he realizes that Willy is not the popular, business-savvy hero whom he spends his youth idolizing; rather, his father is nothing but a "fake" (Miller 1093). Biff's pompous ideology shatters the moment he recognizes that Willy's "I'm vital in New England" attitude is the source of his entire household's hollow pride (Miller 1072). Returning to a family's "recursive nature," Biff's rift from Willy and his subsequent pursuit of "finding himself" take quite a toll on the Lomans' outwardly carefree lifestyle (Miller 1072).

The remainder of the play exposes the tragic results of aspiring to one man's standards of perfection, with each character demonstrating a personal response to Willy's impact. As an adult, Happy seeks compensation for affection denied to him in youth through keeping company with a wide variety of women, persistently ignorant of his and his family's state of crisis. Linda, who at least realizes that "attention must be paid" to Willy's increasing incompetency, remains blinded by her love for her husband and simply cannot bear to "insult" him (Miller 1092, 1094). Though Biff powerfully desires honest communication between his relatives, the tendencies towards irresponsibility and stealing that he develops in adolescence persistently haunt him. Rather than exhibiting any growth whatsoever, Miller's tragic hero, Willy Loman, falls deeper into delusion. Even in the midst of this confused salesman's suicide — Willy's final attempt to make success for the Lomans — the family cannot reach a peaceful consensus as to whether Willy's pristine dream is "the only dream [one] can have" (Miller 1131).

The Lomans spend years complying with Willy's expectations; contrastingly, most members of the Hoover household overtly ridicule Richard's thirst for perfection. The crucial exception is Olive who, in her youthful innocence, cannot yet form her own opinions and consequently looks to her guardians for total guidance. As her father serves as a "teacher, role modeler, and socializer who demonstrate[s] . . . reward[s]s, punish[es], and otherwise shape[s]" Olive, she develops an overwhelming fear of failing (Masten and Shaffer 12). Though the rest of the family is not so easily influenced, they lack any form of unity and coexist in a state of mass confusion "trying to make sense of the world and find a secure and rational place in it" (Laurier). Uncertainty goads family member to construct walls or "boundaries" between themselves and the other family members (Conoley 4). While to an extent boundaries may exist within any ordinary family, the borders marking each Hoover's territory are exceptionally "impermeable," preventing "information, affection, and supervision" from "flow[ing] easily between" them (Conoley 4). Though the family is not exactly enthusiastic about its impending expedition to a "prepubescent" beauty pageant, the Hoovers begin connecting as a family through adversity (Laurier). Diverging from the disastrous outcomes in *Death of a Salesman* and *Little Miss Sunshine*, honest communication between the Hoovers leads to actual unification. As family members observe Olive dance provocatively in the "Little Miss Sunshine" pageant, they realize that their family is far from perfect, but that accepting each member as he or she is is possible. Through their comedic journey of harmonious growth, the Hoovers demonstrate that, although a family may indeed experience a constant array of problems, each member must not only love, but accept the others in order to fully appreciate the joys of family. In the end, the Hoover family escapes the tragic fate of the Lomans to find their own happy ending by way of recognition and acceptance.

Despite their various divergences, both *Death of a Salesman* and *Little Miss Sunshine* attest that the dire consequences of living under false pretenses are far more harmful than being the odd family on the block. This is not to say that the father figures of either drama are wicked men by any means; they are simply befuddled about how to achieve happiness for themselves or within their families. While the "traditional" family still holds respect in modern culture, the problematic family, in turn, finds far greater acceptance than in the era of *Death of a Salesman*. Family dysfunction is actually a common source of amusement for much of today's America, as is prevalent in the hoards of reality television programs focusing on the subject (*Jerry Springer, Wife Swap*, etc.) and the comedic plot of *Little Miss Sunshine*. However, in an era of skyrocketing divorce rates and domestic violence, one begins to wonder at what point acceptance of family imperfection converges with approval of hollow relationships.

Works Cited

Arndt, Michael. *Little Miss Sunshine. Movies Script Place*. 9 Oct. 2003. <http://www.moviescriptplace.com/data/Little%20Miss%20Sunsine.pdf>.

Conoley, Collie W., and Jane Close. *Positive Psychology and Family Therapy: Creative Techniques and Practical Tools for Guiding Change and Enhancing Growth*. Hoboken, New Jersey: John Wiley & Sons, Inc., 2009.

Masten, Ann S., and Anne Shafer. "How Families Matter in Child Develop ment." *Families Count: Effects on Child and Adolescent Development*. Ed. Allison Clarke-Stewart and Judy Dunn. New York: Cambridge University Press, 2006. 5-25.

Laurier, Joanne. "Little Miss Sunshine: High Anxiety." *World Socialist Web site*. 26 Aug. 2006. International Committee of the Fourth International. 9 Nov. 2009. <http://www.wsws.org/articles/2006aug/2006/sun-a26.shtml>.

Miller, Arthur. *Death of a Salesman. Prentice Hall Literature Portfolio*. Ed. Christy Desmet, D. Alexis Hart, and Deborah Church Miller. Upper Saddle River: Pearson Education, Inc., 2007. 1069-1132.

ENGL1102m
Student: Mariana Heredia
Instructor: Cyndi VanderVen

Crime and Punishment—Egyptian Style

Karl Marx's economic ideology explains that as the gap between the rich and the poor increases, a revolution becomes inevitable. The proletariat's lack of everything from power to food leads this larger, poorer class to rebel against the few who have more ("The Communist Manifesto"). It is a game thriving on the jealous instinct of man. The most devious feelings surface in the most savage of manners. This is the situation Sun'allah Ibrahim depicts in his novel *The Committee*. The crime is not the unknown actions of the nameless narrator; this is not important, for Ibrahim gives absolutely no mention of what has occurred. The criminal is not even important. He simply serves as a tool to relate a bigger message about Egyptian society during the 1970s and 1980s. The woman on the old, battered bus, however, depicts the true offense. She, like so many other Egyptians with no money or power, has no say over any part of her life, including the body that moves her from one place to another. Any man can touch her because she does not own herself; thus, the ordinary citizens' lack of power, not only in Egypt, but in a large part of the world, emerges as the real crime. Consequently, the actual delinquents are those who refuse to award equal power, in this case, the government. The result, as Marx predicts, will be a harsh and dangerous revolution.

Ibrahim purposely makes the setting of his novel more important than the main plot in order to chronicle Egyptian society's change in ideology. The narrator explains, "In the '60s the Egyptian market had been restricted to a single car, the Nasser/Fiat, which was assembled in local plants. Now, various imported makes of cars flooded into the market, arriving directly from their home factories" (Ibrahim 128). In this description, Ibrahim demonstrates the change in Egyptian values. Prior to the huge influx of foreign cars, the country had operated on, and consequently valued, a smaller car and a smaller ideology. Afterward, the more money a person possessed, the more successful he/she became. This change also occurred largely because of the election of Anwar El Sadat to the presidency. Part of his agenda included converting Egypt from a closed-off command economy dominated by the public sector to one dominated by private investment (Cheng). The doctor the nameless narrator encounters when he breaks his arm perfectly illustrates the country's obsession with having more money to gain more American products. This man dares to charge an extra pound just for a follow-up visit. The narrator points out that the doctor does not really charge for the medical advice, but instead, he demands more money for the "furniture, the air conditioner, the sound system, and the medical equipment" (Ibrahim 151). The situation really demonstrates the disadvantage the lower class has been put in due to American consumerism. They, like the narrator, simply cannot afford the extra pound; therefore, their health is put at risk. In this situation, the narrator becomes somewhat belligerent because he feels so helpless; however, he has the sense not to act on his helplessness. Although he leaves the doctor's office angry, he makes no real effort to hurt the doctor or his belongings. Other men might not have the same patience, and they might actually act on their anger, destroying the office or even physically hurting the doctor. Such violence did break out in Egypt during the 1970s and 1980s during Sadat's reign. At this time, the government stopped controlling the price of bread and consequently, the prices rose to such a degree that people could not afford their food. The poor public sector turned wild as bread riots broke out in Egypt (Cheng). This is the sort of dangerous revolution Marx warns about. People become so desperate and willing, they inspire a revolution against their oppressors.

In this particular case, the oppressors are those in office since these are the people who refuse to give the lower class the power it deserves. Under ideal circumstances, the government provides protection for its citizens in one main and simple way: it supplies a police force meant to keep each citizen's property safe. This includes the citizens' own bodies. Ibrahim's Egypt sees none of this. For example, in the scene where an angry man with few morals punches the narrator, none of the onlookers think of calling the police to end the fight, but instead, they tell the man, "Calm down. A cat in heat and a fag. Your virility aroused them and they picked a quarrel with you. Why sweat blood over them?" (Ibrahim 148). Had this occurred in the United States, they would not comfort the hostile man. They would have called for the police, but since the police are not a reliable source in Egypt, they settle for calming down the beast. The scene shows what will happen if the government keeps suppressing those in the lower class. The latter will transform from civil people into savages willing to do whatever it takes to get what they want. In this case, the man was willing to assault a woman sexually and punch another man in the face just to satisfy his sexual needs (Ibrahim 147).

Having criminals for a government creates a highly dangerous atmosphere within a country. People may do whatever they want because law and protection do not exist. Consequently, in this situation, the popularity of consumerism has grown to such an extent that the lower class, uninhibited by the lack of a police force, willingly attacks others for a profit. All of this culminates in a rebellion so desperate it turns bloody. Ibrahim's Egypt has not made it to this stage yet, but it is on that path. The narrator describes how he "was able to notice how most of the passersby had caught the urge to seek wealth and happiness. Crates of Coca-Cola were everywhere. Everyone stood behind them, grocers, doorkeepers, carpenters, and even pharmacists" (Ibrahim 136). These now civil citizens will eventually thrive on their need for Coca-Cola and turn violent. They will rush the streets of Egypt, asserting what little power they may have left with brutal force. They will use guns, bombs, anything, just to overthrow those keeping them in ruins. Eventually, Egypt's military assassinated Sadat, and although the people of the country were not involved directly, it is hard to imagine they did not agree with the military's actions. Without such support from the people, it is unlikely that the military would have acted so harshly.

Poverty instills a bitter desperation in the people of the lower class all over the world. They literally starve to death while they watch a select few enjoy fine meals, wear fancy clothes, and drive expensive cars. This sparks a jealousy so blinding that they do not even notice when they commit murder during the revolts. In order to prevent this type of behavior, each government must stop committing its own crime. It must give its people some sort of power through a valid vote. With this, the people can go on to protect their own interests, or at least, their own bodies.

Works Cited

Cheng, Bernard. Egyptian Society Research Paper for English 1102M class. University of Georgia. 2009.

Ibrahim, Sun Allah, and Mary S. St. Germain. *The Committee: A Novel.* Middle East Literature in Translation. Syracuse: Syracuse University Press, 2001.

"The Communist Manifesto." *Wikipedia, The Free Encyclopedia.* 2 Dec. 2009, 03:57 UTC. 3 Dec. 2009. <http://en.wikipedia.org/w/index.php?title=The_Communist_Manifesto&oldid=329178876>.

CHAPTER ELEVEN

Michael G. Moran Electronic Portfolio Awards for 2009-2010

Moran Awards for 2008-2009

Beginning in 2007, the English Department began recognizing the excellent work being done in electronic portfolios for English 1101, 1102, and 1102m by presenting three portfolio awards. Named in honor of Michael G. Moran, a former director of FYC who did much to shape and improve the program and who has continued to support it by serving loyally on the First-year Composition Committee, the awards consist of cash prizes and publication of selected screen shots from the winning ePortfolios in this book. We hope soon to be able to provide public access to these excellent portfolios on the First-year Composition website, as well.

ENGL1101
Student: Trevor Spears
Teacher: Caroline Bartunek

Trevor Spears's Bio and Image:

My name is Trevor Spears. I was born in Ottumwa, Iowa, but I moved to Austin, Texas very quickly. My parents are Tod and Kelly Spears, and I have a younger brother, Colin, who is a freshman in high school. I am the first to attend the University of Georgia in my family. Both of my parents are Oklahoma State University alumni, which will make the first game of this football season

pretty fun. Watching football and playing football is just one of the many things that I enjoy. I love all sorts of outdoor activities and just being outside.

Trevor Spears's Introductory Reflective Essay:

IRE

When first asked if my portfolio had a theme, I could not begin to understand how I was going to throw a paper on the Kings of Leon, the death penalty, and Michael Jordan under one thematic umbrella. Although on the surface there are no common denominators between any of my submissions, it became obvious to me only after further inspection and analysis that I was not trying to express any profound message in my papers. Instead, I came to the realization that through my essays I unknowingly kept a record of what I considered major events in my first semester out on my own. Therefore, I would like my portfolio to be experienced as an unconventional narrative of the fall of my freshman year.

If I am going to go in order of succession, I guess I need to start with my wild card submission, "MJ is My Man." Right around the time we received the writing prompt for our first essay, the National Basketball Association was inducting its newest members into the elite and prestigious Basketball Hall of Fame. Michael Jordan had finally "retired" long enough from basketball to be punching his ticket into the club. ESPN made a big shindig out of it since the greatest basketball player of the last fifty years had finally made it to the proverbial Promised Land. However, things did not go as smoothly as the television executives would have hoped, or maybe it did (everyone loves to watch a train wreck). Unfortunately for MJ during his acceptance speech, he put his size thirteen straight into his mouth and demolished some toes on his way there. His irreverent jabs and egotistical jabs were all the news in the sporting community for a few days. So naturally, I decided to write about how and why Michael Jordan was a hero and a major influence in my life up to this point. In this essay, I really work on not just showing, but telling in my own voice how he was a role model for me.

Growing up, I had a pretty close group of friends. Because everyone had known each other for so long, it was kind of difficult leaving the sense of a secure safe haven that we had built with each other over the years. We decided that the first time we would meet back up with each other would be at Austin City Limits in October. ACL is a three day music festival that mixes big name acts like Pearl Jam and Dave Matthews with relatively unknown artists like Bob Schneider. As school dragged on through August and September, all I could think about was this music festival. Even though there were so many bands playing, I was looking forward to the Kings of Leon the most. Therefore, when asked to write about the influence of a band, television show, or a movie, I chose to write about the Kings of Leon. This essay, "The Kings of Leon Could Care Less," is my first revised essay. Although writing this essay was a challenge because I had to write using interviews as evidence instead of facts from books like I was taught to, I believe that I was able to create what I had gathered into an interesting argument. In this paper, I write about the nonchalant, apathetic attitude towards critics' opinions that the Kings possess and how it is seemingly reflective of today's young people.

Right around the time the third and final essay was assigned my mom had emailed me an article about a death penalty case in the state of Texas. In this case, the man that was convicted of committing a gruesome murder thirty years ago was found innocent with new forensic evidence. This article was big news around Austin, and it got me thinking about the disagreements on the death penalty. In my second revised essay, I present both sides of the controversial issue of capital punishment. This paper was harder to write than I thought it would be because controlling my personal bias on the issue was oddly difficult. However, overall it was worth writing because it forced me to understand both sides of the argument.

My peer review exhibit and my own revision exhibit show the skills that I have developed throughout this semester. In both of these exhibits, I focus on sentence structure, diction, and grammar. I feel as if both of these exhibits display the writing skills I have developed throughout this course.

Trevor Spears's Wild Card Exhibit

MJ is My Man

When I say MJ, I am not referring to the recently deceased King of Pop. Although Michael Jackson was a great musician, there is, however, a greater MJ that I am talking about. He is a man who tried his hand in a variety of areas. He dabbled on the baseball diamond, although it was minor leagues; he ruled the big screen with Bugs Bunny in *Space Jam;* and he will always be remembered as the king of the basketball court. I am talking about no one other than the great Michael Jordan. Along with every other boy my age, Michael was my hero. Let's be honest for a second, what little boy growing up in the 1990s did not look up to MJ? He had it all: the NBA championships, the MVP's, even his own brand of shoes. Number twenty-three inspired kids everywhere to grab a ball and find the nearest court, whether it be asphalt, wood, or gravel, and just play for the love of the game. However, as I grew older, my idolization of Michael Jordan drastically changed. My obsession had matured from modeling my playing style after the player on the court to looking up to the man beyond all of the glory. Many do not consider Michael the best role model because of certain character deficiencies, but I believe that these character flaws are actually what made Michael Jordan one of the biggest inspirations in my life.

Being born in the Midwest, my love for basketball seems to have been an evolutionary trait necessary for me to survive in the land of cornfields and *Hoosiers*. If one was a boy growing up in this region of the country, he loved basketball no matter what. One would follow college hoops, especially professional ball, and even high school basketball. One would wait in line for what seemed like hours wasting valuable recess time on the playground in order to get a little bit of precious time on the court. The only problem was that if you weren't any good, this valuable time you waited so long for would be very short lived. Therefore, many kids modeled their type of playing style after major NBA stars. On any given blacktop court, you could find self-proclaimed Charles Barkleys, Scottie Pippins's, and a ton of Michael Jordans. This is where my original obsession with Michael Jordan developed. I decided that if I was going to be a player, I wanted to be the best. I would spend hours in our gravel driveway holding my own practices. I would slash to the basket trying to switch hands mid-layup, each time sticking my tongue out so I could be exactly "like Mike." I worked my ass off practicing that fade-away jumper he had down to an art form to hand so many teams last second defeats. Thus, the first thing that Michael, along with my dad, taught me was the discipline of practice and working hard. Looking back, my dad taught me most of the benefits of working hard, but Air Jordan was the inspiration. I would have never done it if I hadn't wanted to be exactly like Michael.

After I had practiced my game enough and I felt that I sufficiently possessed certain aspects of the arsenal of MJ, I took my game to the court with the older guys. I did this because I had read in a *Sports Illustrated* or some sort of Michael spotlight article that he had grown up playing on the court with his older brothers and their friends, and since I had no older brothers I decided to go there by myself. That first day at the park, I was so intimidated. I felt so tiny and weak next to those guys, but when the game started all of that seemed to disappear. I just played my game and had fun. I would like to say that I dropped 69 points, like Michael did against Cleveland, but truth was I went maybe three for seven. By no means was it a spectacular performance, but it was good enough for them to respect me and invite me back. The more I played ball with those guys, the better friends I became with them. I ended up finding one of my best friends, Levi, in that group of guys. Yeah, we bonded over basketball and how great Michael was, but our friendship was more than that. He was the type of guy who was always there for me no matter what. I can only attribute the start of this friendship to Michael. MJ had inspired a certain self confidence in me that I had never felt before. Thanks to him, I was confident enough to step out of my comfort zone and be my own person around the older guys, consequently making one of my best friends.

Around the time I was about thirteen or fourteen, I started reading the intensive biographies about Michael Jordan and the skeletons in his closet. I learned, in detail, for the first time about how the death of his father had affected his career and his personal life. I learned that his mourning had taken form in a horrible gambling problem. He had ended up putting his career on hold because of these extenuating circumstances. I struggled with understanding how the greatest basketball player could let an off-court drama take him away from the game that he loved. Finding this new information out, I definitely took him off the pedestal a little bit. MJ was still my hero, but for the first time I looked at Michael as an example of what not to do. Michael's stumble was just the reminder I needed when my grandmother passed away my junior year of high school. I found that dealing with the grief was extremely difficult for me. She was a woman who was another huge influence in my life. It would have been easy for me to look for complete refuge and comfort in things that would temporarily take the pain away, but I remembered Michael and how his inability to cope with his emotions took him away from one of the things he held most dear. His bad example had become my shining example, and MJ helped steer me away from a path that I had already set out on.

As I have grown older and older, I have learned more about who Michael Jordan is as a man off the court. Although the player MJ inspired me to work hard, be poised, and be confident, it is the man Michael Jordan that has inspired me to be someone better than myself. He inspired me to be a better man by showing me his true character when I had the opportunity to meet my hero on a golf course in Austin at about age fifteen. I was able to meet Michael in the clubhouse after his round of golf and I got his autograph and all that useless stuff, but what I really wanted was to just talk to him for a few minutes about what a hero he had been to me growing up. I never got this chance. He didn't even look up when he signed his rookie card; he just shrugged me off and pretended like he didn't hear me. I know he was probably busy and had places to go, but there weren't more than seven people in that room, and he didn't even give me the time of day. This was excusable because he was/is one of the most popular basketball players of all time. However, the dagger to the heart was seeing how he treated the people around him. MJ was just downright rude to the people working at the golf course and the people working for him. He treated them as if they barely existed in this world and that their whole reason for existence was to take care of him. After seeing this display of arrogance and disrespect, I promised myself that no matter how successful I became I would never treat people any differently.

Despite all of my efforts when I was younger, I was never going to be Michael Jordan or even the next Michael Jordan. Now, I don't want to be anything like Michael Jordan. However, even through his downfalls and deficiencies, Michael Jordan has been a great inspiration for me because he has helped me find my own way. Yes, MJ is still the man, but in my opinion he is not a man that I want to be like in every aspect of my life. I was able to learn from his character flaws and discover for myself what type of person I want to become. Without Michael as an inspiration, there are valuable life lessons I would never have wanted to learn, varying from the benefits of focus to the importance of humility. Therefore, through the good and the bad, I am immensely thankful for the unknowing role MJ has played in my life.

Trevor Spears's Revision Exhibit

When I revise a paper, I carefully inspect all aspects of my work. I look at grammar, sentence structure, and organization. Often, my first draft looks like a skeleton compared to my final product. Revising really helps me inspect my paper from top to bottom. The second essay I wrote on the Kings of Leon is a very strong example of the changes I make while revising my work. Below is the second paragraph of this essay, and I will take you through the steps I went through while revising this paragraph.

First Version:

Since the Kings of Leon's existence, their music has evolved into a sound that is uniquely their own. When the band started in 1999, only two of the four members had ever touched an instrument before, which ~~lead~~ to what many music magazines described as a sound that possessed a southern drawl and a garage band twist to a music style similar to 1970's rock (NME). However, as the albums have progressed, the Kings of Leon have moved away from the garage band sound that they built their roots on and have developed a more stadium rock sound. Although many critics say that the band has just changed their sound in order to sell albums, the Kings stand by their music in multiple interviews saying that "there's no formula for us, as far as songwriting goes" and that their new sound is derived from them "growing from day one"(Puremusic 2). The band says that they are not concerned if people like their music or not and believe that them not caring has given them the freedom to express themselves in whatever way they so choose (Puremusic). Many people say that the band's perceived freedom from critics has played a major role in the boys finding a sound that is uniquely Kings of Leon.

This first version is basically the framework that I build on for my final product. I try to use the first go around to organize my thoughts and begin to form my argument. I mainly focus on how I am going to use my evidence, and I deal with my grammatical errors when I revise it.

Second Version:

Since the beginning, the Kings of Leon's music has evolved into a sound that is uniquely their own. When the band started in 1999, only two of the four members had ever touched instruments before, which ~~led~~ to what many music magazines described as a sound that possessed a southern drawl and a garage band twist to a music style similar to 1970's rock ("Kings of Leon: Aha Shake Heartbreak"). They have released four albums: Youth and Young Manhood (2003), Aha Shake Heartbreak (2004), Because of the Times (2006), and Only by the Night (2008). As these albums have been released, the Kings of Leon have moved away from the garage band sound that was very prevalent on the earlier releases and have developed a sound that is reminiscent of 1980's arena rock. With the change in music, many critics say that the band has just altered their sound in order to appeal to the masses. However, the Kings adamantly claim that the music they are making is authentic to them. In multiple interviews, such as the one with Puremusic.Com, the band stands by their music saying that "there's no formula for us, as far as songwriting goes" and that they make music that is real to them ("A Conversation with Nathan Followill"). The Kings of Leon also believe that this evolution is a byproduct of their maturation as a band and consider themselves "growing from day one" ("A Conversation with Nathan Followill"). They feel that this growth has only been able to occur because they are not concerned if people like their music, which has ultimately led to them being able to produce a sound that they consider genuinely theirs ("A Conversation with Nathan Followill").

In this second version, I made many revisions. I corrected the misspelling of "lead" to "led." The blue highlighted sentences are additions that I made, whether small details or full sentences. Every addition I made put more "meat" on the bones of my original paragraph. The yellow highlighted areas are the sentences in which I changed the wording and the structure. All of these sentences highlighted needed to be corrected in order to make the paragraph have a stronger voice and a smoother flow. Every correction I made to this paragraph was needed in order to produce a final product that was an error free and logical argument.

ENGL1102
Student: Katie Ali Farhani
Teacher: Sara Amis

Katie Ali Farhani's Bio and Image:

**Picture of me and my family at one of our reunions. I am the one in the middle of the front row (between my grandparents on the rocking chairs) with the dark hair. I absolutely love my family.

I, Katie AliFarhani, was born in Columbus, Georgia to an Iranian father and an American mother on May 23, 1991 at 10:43 pm. Being the lucky one, I was the baby of the batch of five and also the only girl. Yes, that's right, I have four older brothers. They are most likely responsible for my aggressiveness and ability to protect myself and my beliefs.

Though my picture might seem like a typical American family, there is a completely different side that is not shown. My dad (seen in the far left corner) has family that currently lives in Iran. Therefore, I might seem like a typical "white" female on the outside, but I am actually half Iranian and a mix of many different backgrounds. I can be over-analytical, complicated, yet be very outgoing and simple; the latter two are what I consider the better traits, of course.

I'm proud of my heritage and my religion. Being a Muslim in Georgia has definitely made me a stronger person. I have had to fight against stereotypical remarks, especially after September 11th. But this negativity has also resulted in positivity. I have opened the eyes of many people who didn't realize the truth about the Middle East and Islam. I have also been affiliated with many organizations that promote spreading the acceptance of diversity, and I even received a scholarship for doing so. I think my background has a lot to do with why I want to help those in need. I aspire to teach others how to accept diversity and live in harmony with others who are different from themselves. I think that people should work towards having better communication and a greater understanding of others. I believe if two opposing parties would simply sit down and respectfully discuss their differences, they would soon realize that the conflicts between them can be simplified into a more understandable matter.

Katie Ali Farhani's Introductory Reflective Essay

Diversity and the Writing Process: My Introductory Reflective Essay

Regardless of our location, we are surrounded by diversity. Different points of view, different backgrounds, different personalities, and so on. Each of these concepts forms who we are and is shown through our different styles of writing. Because of my diverse background and my religion (Islam), I've been confronted many times by curious people who either want to know more about the Middle East and Islam, or feel as if they are obligated to tell me that I am wrong or am a "terrorist." After going to a Christian school for almost ten years and being exposed to many different religions, I have been prepared to face challenges. When compared to writing an essay, this can be seen as my "evidence" that I've researched. Everyone knows that in writing, you must always consider other points of view and be able to back up your thoughts with evidence. However, my writing, like me, can be complex and at times confusing, but I've been striving for quite some time to simplify both my life and my writing. After confronting many people with opposing views, I realized that giving them extensive, drawn out information usually distracts them from the main point. Instead, it's best to give them concise, simple evidence, especially at first, to catch their attention and make them think about the topic at hand. This perfectly correlates to what I realized about writing in my English 1102 class. I initially lacked the ability to simplify my thoughts, but after peer reviews, lectures, and revisions on how to do so, I was able to improve my way of writing, which can be seen throughout my portfolio.

I consider my strengths to be analyzing a piece and interpreting the writer's style in order to propose a certain idea. I tend to write about how those who are "superior could have something in common with those who are labeled inferior." I also strive to give a voice to those who are not usually given the opportunity to speak, both in my writing and in real life situations. This can be seen through my analysis of Maya Angelou's "Still I Rise" poem, in which I point out certain literary devices and how they intertwine to strengthen Angelou's purpose of the poem. This can also be seen in my first essay, which involved more research than the second. Though researching is not exactly my forte, my first essay shows how I learned to gather evidence from outside sources to fit into the meaning of my essay. For example, I used three critics' opinions on Kate Chopin's "Désirée's Baby" to formulate a conclusion how "Chopin's juxtaposition of light and dark emphasizes the intended theme of anti-racism." Another strength and weakness of mine is grammar and diction editing; I can usually find the most proper way of saying things that only have a simplistic idea behind them. While this is exceptional for peer reviewing, it is at times harsh on me when I sit for fifteen minutes simply trying to find the perfect way to write down my ideas on paper. I can be considered a perfectionist when it comes to this aspect, but one major thing I have recently learned is to simply get the idea down and focus on how strong it is, instead of worrying about how elegantly it can be presented.

Usually, it is difficult for me to put everything together and mold my thoughts into a seemingly excellent essay. But through my teacher's and classmates' comments, I was able to revise my essays to accurately present my thoughts. One can see this in my revision exhibit and in my first essay's conclusion, in which I simplified a weak, confusing conclusion—"Chopin addresses the color issues that were occurring during the antebellum time and inadvertently explicates the effects of hastily concluding one's status in society. Her story confirms that racism is not only based on skin color but also depends upon one's mindset and aura" — into a more understandable and concise thought: "Chopin addresses the color issues that were occurring during the antebellum period and shows the effects of hastily determining one's status in society. Her story confirms that racism is not only based on skin color and appearance but also inherently in the eye of the racist." In this example, like many others throughout my portfolio, I combined my complex way of writing with the intended simplicity of thoughts.

I especially realized the importance of simplicity in my English 1102 class. In my IB high school classes, I was taught to present ideas elegantly and sternly. However, after seeing classmates' essays and how well they did when writing informally, I realized how casual and simplistic our writing could be. By peer reviewing, one can see the different points of view and ways of writing. It gives us the opportunity to show our strengths and help others' weaknesses. Peer reviewing countless essays and talking with classmates helped me and my peers shape a more effective way to write.

My Wild Card seems completely different than everything in my portfolio. However, it shows my ability to compromise and have some fun with creative, "out of the box" ideas. By doing a group project (my Wild Card), I learned how difficult circumstances involving varied personalities can create a great product. This, along with peer reviewing, can be related to everyday life; two opposing parties could be arguing and overruling the other's opinion, which in a way is like peer reviewing, except more harsh, of course. Like learning to come to a consensus in a paper, one could compromise in life when faced with a problem. The diversity of the two parties can then be seen as a positive aspect instead of negative, which would allow, with proper attitude, an effective conclusion.

Compromise. Simplicity. Diversity. Each of these different ideas can be linked to one another to form a chain of progress. While these concepts are at times difficult to correlate, sharing thoughts and ideas while being respectful can lead to the greatest of outcomes. One can correlate writing and literature to appreciating others' points of view and diversities. Instead of making a situation more complex than it already seems, like how I initially did in my writing, figuring out an easier and more effective way of sharing ideas is key. Overall, writing is like overcoming diversity. Once a person presents his ideas, he has to consider the way in which he presents them, the effect on the audience, as well as the response he will provoke.

Katie Ali Farhani's Revision Exhibit

When we were assigned a poetry project, I instantly looked for a poem that spoke out to me. My absolute favorite author is Maya Angelou, and luckily I found a poem by her in our book. The poem I chose is "Still I Rise," which is an inspirational poem about overcoming adversity and prevailing regardless of what troubles may come. The following excerpt is from my final draft which was graded by my teacher. She highlighted this sentence and said that the diction was awkward, which I agreed with fully because I remember struggling to find the correct wording. The sentence is in the end of one of the body paragraphs and was meant to be a strong sentence to emphasize Angelou's style.

Though this stanza comprises **sad expressions, the** underlying tone can still be seen as arising and strengthening **through the way** Angelou presents the negativity.

When I first looked at this sentence after receiving my teacher's comments, I realized that it seems very complex and confusing, which is something that I have struggled with in my writing. I knew what I was trying to say but it was extremely difficult to write it down in a way that explained my thoughts exactly. So, what I first did was simplify the sentence by taking out "comprises" and adding "is full of." The next step I took was brainstorming about what words I was looking for that could correctly explain the tone. After a few minutes, I realized that "hopeful" would be the best way to describe the tone. Therefore "arising and strengthening" has been modified to simply "hopeful." Next, I noticed that I needed to change the last part of the sentence. I realized that I could change "Angelou presents the negativity" into saying "Angelou presents them," with "them" being the pronoun antecedent for the sad expressions. So, I put the last part of the sentence first and added my changes to come up with my final, simplified version:

Though this stanza is full of **sad expressions, Angelou presents** them **in a way that still creates a** hopeful **tone.**

Revision is always helpful, especially after one receives comments from teachers or classmates on certain points of the essay. By realizing that this sentence also seemed awkward and confusing to another individual, I decided to simplify it and directly present my ideas. I felt that the more I write, the more clear my points would become, but I discovered that this process usually leads to more confusion, something that I was trying to avoid. Simplicity is something that I have learned to use throughout my writing process this semester. Therefore, I think that this revision exhibit shows how I have overcome my struggles with flowery writing and learned to produce something simpler and concise.

Katie Ali Farhani's Peer Review Exhibit

When my classmates and I first had to peer-review in middle school, the first thing we said to each other was, "Don't make me look stupid!" However, I realized over the years that peer-reviewing wasn't meant for us to be a rude, overly critical reviewer to make ourselves seem smarter, but instead it was meant to help the other person improve their writing. I also realized that I could learn from others' mistakes when I peer-reviewed their essays. It was especially helpful to review and gather how my classmates wrote in my English 1102 class, because I felt as if I was writing too "flowery." Therefore, peer reviewing benefits both the commentator and the writer with better brainstorming information and helps form a medium between others' advice and personal thought. I chose these paragraphs as my peer review examples because they show how I used what I learned in high school to critique other papers: taking out information I thought wasn't needed ("trimming the fat" as my Senior English teacher told me), simplifying ideas, and further explaining ideas with literary examples in order not to confuse the audience.

[1]During the time period, **Armand held a prestigious title among the town that** [2]he was not willing to give up **for the love of his wife. The enterprise of keeping his family name is** [3]remissible **in the** [4]literary time period, **considering large amounts of pressure were put on the family to** [5]stay on their toes **throughout hard times**.

1 & 4) You need to specify exactly what time period.

2 & 5) These two phrases seem very colloquial and informal; maybe change to something more formal, such as "survive" for 5?

3) Wrong word

In this exhibit, this writer was pointing out the severity of Armand's actions in "Desiree's Baby" when he dismissed his wife and baby. In this example, she does not specify the time period in which the story takes place, which is an important factor in why he acted how he did. She also uses very vague and informal terms, which I was taught not to write. These comments were helpful for her to narrow down her points and state concisely what she means. The next example is the conclusion of her essay that I also reviewed:

The [7]disownment **of Desiree and the baby displays the selfishness that Armand embodies. Leaving a wife and child to continue their lives without a father figure**[8] poses future psychological and emotional problems in lives of the family. **To me, a current life is more salient than a family name would be. My opinion has been swayed by culture differences in the current time period compared to the literature time period.** [9]In those times, it is plausible that a honorable family name could hold more prominence and the continued exaltation could be worth more than a single quandary in the system. **Either way, the abandonment of Desiree and the baby portrayed a nauseating scene to endure.**[10]

7) Wrong word

8) You probably don't need this information

9) "a honorable family" needs to be changed to "an honorable family," and the sentence seems very awkward and complex . . . It's difficult to understand exactly what you're trying to conclude.

10) You need to have more evidence and form a concise opinion and conclusion. You end on a "either way" note, but you need to set a firm opinion and use more evidence from the book or critics rather than your own personal experience. Keep it literary. But overall good job!

I critiqued this paragraph very closely because I felt a conclusion should be very precise and clear. She again struggled to find the right word, as I and many writers do. I also noted phrases that probably didn't need to be included because they seemed to represent a completely different idea. The entire essay seemed to be strictly from her views and beliefs, which is good to have in an essay; however, I also noted that it doesn't need to strictly be about this; she needed to add more literary analysis. I added a "good job!" at the end to continue motivating her to finish a strong, good quality essay, which she continued to do. I chose each of these examples to show my skills in closely analyzing a classmate's paper and helping her "trim the fat" with unnecessary details. These examples also illuminate my skills in grammar/diction editing, which I do meticulously. However, I learned after editing this paper, as well as others, that I needed to lessen the intensity of elaborate language in my essays.

Katie Ali Farhani's Wild Card Exhibit

My Humorous, Entertaining Wild Card

Hand Puppet Hamlet
http://www.youtube.com/watch?v=DY5HG4HpPKM

Above is a link to my group's video on YouTube, which we did for an extra credit project in my English 1102 class. We decided to do a quick, funny synopsis of *Hamlet* by using hand puppets. We came up with this idea when one of our group members was playing around and talking with his hand. We then each contributed to the production of the "play." I was the camera woman because I was not too skilled in hand puppetry, and I had the better quality camera. I also contributed to ideas in production and editing. Personally, I think this video provides a funny, creative side to me and my portfolio.

ENGL 1102M
Student: Teneil Salmon
Teacher: Alison Lenhardt

Teneil Salmon's Bio and Image:

Teneil Anesia Salmon was born on a tropical island in the Caribbean called Jamaica. For seventeen years, Teneil was raised in a country with its roots embedded in the African, Spanish, and British cultures. For the first two years of her life, she was raised in a bustling town called St. Catherine, but her family moved to the cool hills of Manchester in 1991. During her childhood and adolescent years in Manchester, Teneil learned about her African background and developed an appreciation for the folk songs, traditional dishes, and customs that collectively define her country's unique culture.

During the holidays, Teneil enjoyed visiting her relatives, who lived in different regions of the small island. However, her most exciting and memorable vacations were spent at the home of her late grandparents. Her grandparents owned several acres of land, on which they grew a variety of tropical fruits and vegetables that they sold in the market on Saturdays. This land was inherited from her great-grandparents, who lived during the era in which the British ruled the island. Teneil's parents often shared childhood stories about being raised on such a vast amount of land; these stories contributed to Teneil's desire to spend holidays with her grandparents whenever possible. Given the opportunity to spend such valuable time with her grandparents, Teneil was able to learn interesting facts about her family, such as the fact that her grandfather was the first person to own an automobile in his town. Though this fact seemed inconsequential initially, Teneil soon realized that it was an important aspect of her family's history that would be remembered by many residents in her grandparents' community.

In April 2007, Teneil and her family migrated to the United States of America. Despite this change in location, Teneil remained fully aware of her background and has always been willing to share her culture with those around her. She has resided in the United States of America for two years, and she has discovered that there are similarities between both cultures. As a result, the transition into a foreign culture was not as difficult as she perceived initially. She has learned to accept a new culture but has simultaneously preserved the culture of her homeland within her immediate family. Teneil is elated to reside in a country that encourages diversification and looks forward to continue discovering new aspects of its culture.

Teneil Salmon's Introductory Reflective Essay:

The Gradual Improvement of My Craft

Throughout the semester, I was exposed to an array of literary pieces by writers of various ethnicities. By effectively incorporating historical content about their ethnic background into their writings, these writers provided me with insight into the lives of a diverse group of people. Although my classmates and I primarily discussed the content of the literary works, we were also introduced to various writing techniques. As I analyzed the pieces, I realized that writing is truly an artistic form that gives individuals the opportunity to express their dreams and opinions in the form of poetry or prose. Each writer also exhibited exemplary writing skills in areas such as audience awareness and the overall organization of their work. Consequently, I am gradually improving my writing skills so that I can become a more effective writer. The exhibits that are presented in this portfolio demonstrate my improvement in the development of my thesis statements and topic sentences, and in the variation of my sentence structures.

As the semester progressed, I worked meticulously to formulate thesis statements that clearly and specifically stated my argument in a concise manner. At the beginning of the semester, my instructor and peers noted that the thesis statement in my first paper, entitled "Embracing One's Roots," was too vague and needed to be tailored into more concise language. For instance, the following excerpt from Draft One of my Revision Process illustrates these weaknesses in my thesis statement:

> From an in depth analysis of both stories, one can surmise that even though an individual may become more appreciative of his or her heritage because of new experiences endured as time progresses, his or her understanding and appreciation of heritage will vary based on the nature of those experiences.

In order to improve the thesis statement presented above, I tried to elaborate on the italicized portion of my thesis statement by including the names of the characters to be discussed and expounding on the "experiences" that they encountered. The excerpt below illustrates how I learned to develop my thesis statement more effectively:

> Although "The Invisible Man" and Dee become more appreciative of heritage, his or her understanding and appreciation of heritage varies because of the differences in each character's path to cultural appreciation, and the influence of different perspectives on the advancement of African Americans during each character's respective time period.

This revised thesis statement clearly states the points that will be addressed in the body of the paper and demonstrates significant improvement in the overall presentation of my argument. Although there are apparent improvements in my thesis statement, I am aware that there is room for additional improvement. For instance, my argument could be stated more concisely. As I continued writing, I improved on my areas of weakness by formulating my thesis statement before writing my paper and then reviewing it after constructing the paper to ensure that my argument has been stated clearly. I believe that this technique, in addition to the comments made by my instructor and peers, has been instrumental in the development of my thesis statements.

In addition to forming specific thesis statements, I have also become more competent in constructing topic sentences that are specific and maintain the essay's cohesiveness. Similar to my thesis statements at the beginning of the semester, my topic sentences tended to be very vague. The following topic sentence from Revised Essay Two, entitled "The Journey to Prosperity," illustrates this weakness in my writing: "The persona reveals the causes of the women's journey [and *elaborates on the current stage of the women's journey]*." During a conference with my instructor, she noted that the italicized portion of my topic sentence needed to "be more specific." After reviewing the corresponding paragraph and determining its main points, I reconstructed my topic sentence so that it clearly stated the points that would be addressed in the body of the paragraph. The following example from "The Journey to Prosperity" is an accurate reflection of my improvement: "In the poem's final stanza, the speaker reveals that the women's journey is a result of their desire to eradicate poverty in their lives." My instructor and peer reviewers also advised me to ensure that my topic sentences had direct correlation to the content of my paragraphs and my thesis statement. In order to ensure that my topic sentences and thesis statement maintained the paper's coherence, I revised my drafts and ensured that my topic sentences were composed of points that were directly related to my thesis. As the semester progressed, this technique helped to improve my topic sentences thus improving my paper's coherence.

As I made improvements in the development of my thesis statement and topic sentences, I also worked on varying my sentence structure. Throughout the semester, my peers and instructor commented that I had a tendency to overuse introductory clauses to transition from one sentence to another. For instance, the following excerpt from "From Los Vendidos to Di Jamaican Dem" shows my consecutive use of introductory clauses and phrases as transitions:

> Furthermore, while several groups have chosen to perform the play as it was originally scripted, some directors and producers have chosen to alter the ending of the play. . . For instance, when the play was produced by director Jorge Huertas. . . he changed the ending from the original version. . . In fact, the original director and playwright. . . changed the ending of the play. . . In the television version, "a scientist masterminds the operation." (Revised Essay One)

Prior to English 1102M, I was oblivious to the fact that my writing was bombarded with numerous clauses. Once my peers and instructor explained that an excessive incorporation of introductory clauses made my writing monotonous, I worked assiduously throughout the semester on this particular weakness. By following the guidelines and adhering to my peers' suggestions, I was able to develop my paragraphs using a variety of sentence structures as illustrated by the following excerpt from "The Journey to Prosperity":

> The persona primarily speaks of the length of time that the women spend on the streets of Harlem and emphasizes that prostitution lasts "through the long night until the single break of day" . . . The phrase is also a metaphorical comparison to the women's life. To establish that prostitution lasted throughout every season, the persona uses phrases such as "snow-flake" and "earth's white breast." (Revised Essay Two)

The excerpt demonstrates more variation in my sentence structures. Although I did not use introductory clauses or phrases, I maintained the overall flow of the paragraph, which illustrates that I do not have to rely on such devices to improve the quality of my writing.

During the semester, I made significant improvements in my writing which have made me a more proficient writer. With the continuous advice of my instructor and the constructive criticism of my peers, I was able to identify the areas in my writing that I needed to focus on throughout the semester. I also believe that I have become a better peer reviewer, because I am more aware of how to improve certain flaws in the writing process. For instance, in my Peer Review Exhibit I focused on ensuring that my peers' thesis statements and topic sentences were specific, and I also ensured that their sentences were well-constructed. These comments were made in addition to comments on my peers' grammar usage, coherence, and organization. I believe that the combination of my peers' comments and my instructor's advice were not only beneficial to me but also to those whom I assisted.

My writing experience in English 1102M has definitely been rewarding, as I have become a more adept writer. By utilizing the advice of others and learning from my mistakes, I have continued to grow as a writer. I believe that through continuous practice and by applying the knowledge I have learned during this semester, my successive writing assignments will illustrate distinctiveness in thought and technique.

Teneil Salmon's Revision Exhibit

Practice Makes Perfect

In the following Revision Process, I have provided a detailed description of the steps that were taken to construct an effective introductory paragraph and body paragraph. The Revision Process sample was compiled from the first writing assignment that was given this semester. The purpose of the assignment was to compare and contrast the theme of heritage in Ralph Ellison's "Battle Royal" and Alice Walker's "Everyday Use." Throughout my revision process, I made numerous changes to the content, punctuation, grammar, and sentence structure of the paragraphs, which resulted in a more cohesive and coherent paper.

The general steps that were taken during the construction of these paragraphs and the writing assignment as a whole included:

(1) Formulating a draft

(2) Proofreading for errors

(3) Submitting a draft for peer review

(4) Editing the paper based on the comments made by my peers

(5) Discussing additional changes with my instructor

(6) Making additional changes based on the instructor's comments

(7) Proofreading for additional mistakes

(8) Making final changes, if necessary.

The key for the color scheme is as follows:

Portion to be revised

Revised Portions

The Revision Process is as follows:

Draft One

In essence, one's heritage is an indispensable aspect of one's life. However, whether one chooses to embrace one's heritage in its entirety is essentially based on one's personal values, beliefs and experiences. *As a result,* each individual may choose to embrace his or her heritage at different stages in life. Regardless of the point in time in which an individual becomes mindful of his or her heritage, it is safe to assume that most individuals ultimately develop an appreciation for their culture. *Consequently*, in Ralph Ellison's "Battle Royal" and Alice Walker's "Everyday Use," the general concept of appreciating one's heritage forms the basis of each story. In "Battle Royal," it is evident that the narrator develops a greater appreciation for his African American heritage, as is the situation with the character, Dee, in "Everyday Use." *However*, the most captivating aspect of each character's newfound appreciation is the contrast between each character's process of becoming appreciative and the distinctiveness between their resulting attitude. From an in depth analysis of both stories, one can surmise that even though an individual may become more appreciative of his or her heritage because of new experiences endured as time progresses, his or her understanding and appreciation of heritage will vary based on the nature of those experiences.

Even though the narrator in "Battle Royal" and the character, Dee from "Everyday Use" have both learned to embrace their heritage, there is a contrast between how each character develops an appreciation for his or her heritage. In "Battle Royal," the reader instant-

Comment [Teneil]: The opening sentences are unnecessary generalization. My opening sentences should address the subject of the paper directly.

Comment [Teneil]: This phrase is unnecessary.

Comment [Teneil]: This phrase is also unnecessary and may portray a negative tone.

Comment [Teneil]: The thesis statement needs to be more specific. What does "the nature of those experiences" specifically address?

Comment [Teneil]: This phrase can be rewritten as one word.

ly becomes aware of the narrator's initial perception of shame for his heritage when he overtly states: "I am not ashamed of my grandparents for having been slaves. I am only ashamed of myself for having at one time been ashamed" (Ellison 227). *However*, as the narrator describes his experience of unjust treatment and social inequality, one begins to witness his change in attitude. Though not explicitly stated by the narrator, it is apparent that being misled into partaking in the battle royal had a short term and long term effect on his decision to remain bounded by social inequality. It is clear that the narrator has been struggling with the decision of whether or not he should openly embrace his heritage in a society in which African American's are viewed as inferior to the white man and have the "social responsibility" to remain submissive to their superior culture as revealed by the narrator when he exerts that African Americans should "[c]ast down [their] bucket...in making friends in every manly way of the people of all races by whom [they] are all surrounded" (Ellison 234). *However*, it is obvious that the abuse that he endures from the white men has subconsciously affected him which leads him to utter the forbidden words: "social equality" within their midst (Ellison 235). *Undoubtedly*, the narrator's horrid experiences have gradually molded him into an individual who has become more appreciative of his heritage.

Comment [Teneil]: I need to explain what the "short term" and "long term" effects are so that my statement is more specific. I also have the option of deleting this sentence because it does not have a strong relationship to the topic sentence.

Comment [Teneil]: This phrase is unnecessary and sets the stage for a negative tone.

<u>Notes of Revision for Draft One</u>

Based on the comments made above, most of the revision for the first draft involved changes in content. The opening sentences of the paragraph were unnecessary generalizations that were not captivating to my audience. During my writing process, I also discovered that I had a tendency to overuse introductory clauses, which have been italicized in the draft above. Another area of concern is effective construction of a specific thesis statement. Throughout my writing process, I noticed that my thesis statements were too general. As a result, I had to ensure that I revised my thesis statement numerous times so that it presented a clear and specific argument for my paper. For the second paragraph, I focused on sentence structure and ensured that my ideas related to my thesis statement and topic sentence.

Draft Two

In Ralph Ellison's "Battle Royal" and Alice Walker's "Everyday Use", the narrators develop their stories on the notion that heritage is an indispensable aspect of one's life. Through the roles of the characters , they demonstrate that whether one chooses to embrace one's heritage in its entirety is essentially based on one's personal values, beliefs and experiences. *Furthermore*, Ellison and Walker show that each individual may choose to embrace his or her heritage at different stages in life and thus because develop an appreciation for his or her culture. In "Battle Royal", it is evident that the narrator–'The Invisible Man' – develops a greater appreciation for his African American heritage, as is the situation with the character, Dee, in "Everyday Use"[4]. *However*, the most captivating aspect of each character's newfound appreciation is the contrast between each character's process of becoming appreciative and the distinctiveness between their resulting attitude. From an in depth analysis of both stories, one can surmise that even though 'The Invisible Man' and Dee may become more appreciative of their heritage because of new experiences endured as time progresses, his or her

Comment [Teneil]: The opening sentence is more specific to the stories and thus is more effective than unnecessary generalizations.

Comment [Teneil]: The term "they" is unspecific.

Comment [Teneil]: Incorrect grammar usage. The sentences needs to be revised so that the message being portrayed is effectively related to the reader.

Comment [Teneil]: The structure of this sentence needs to be revised because of its awkward wording and wordiness.

understanding and appreciation of heritage will vary based on the nature of those experiences.

Comment [Teneil]: The thesis statement still needs to be revised to reflect a more specific argument

Although the narrator in "Battle Royal" and the character, Dee from "Everyday Use" have both learned to embrace their heritage, there is a contrast between how each character develops an appreciation for his or her heritage. In "Battle Royal", the reader instantly becomes aware of the narrator's initial perception of shame for his heritage, before experiencing the hardships of being an African American, when he overtly states: "I am not ashamed of my grandparents for having been slaves. I am only ashamed of myself for having at one time been ashamed" (Ellison 227). *However*, as the narrator describes his experience of unjust treatment and social inequality, one begins to witness his change in attitude. It is clear that the narrator has been struggling with the decision of whether or not he should openly embrace his heritage in a society in which African American's are viewed as inferior to the white man and have the "social responsibility" to remain submissive to their superior culture as revealed by the narrator when he exerts that African Americans should "[c]ast down [their] bucket...in making friends in every manly way of the people of all races by whom [they] are all surrounded" (Ellison 234). However, the abuse that he endures from the white men has subconsciously affected him which leads him to utter the forbidden words: "social equality" within their midst (Ellison 235). Undoubtedly, the narrator's horrid experiences have gradually molded him into an individual who has become more appreciative of his heritage.

Comment [Teneil]: I need to expound on the narrator's "change in attitude". What was the narrator's initial attitude? Did his attitude change as the story progressed? What evidence from the book supports this change?

Comment [Teneil]: The ideas presented in these sentences should be addressed in an additional paragraph. Once I formulate a new paragraph, I need to incorporate historical information on Booker T. Washington and relate my findings to my ideas as it pertains to the protagonist in "Battle Royal".

Comments on Draft Two

The second draft of the introduction showed several improvements. The opening sentence was more specific to the stories and there was a reduction in the use of introductory clauses. Despite these improvements, a few of the sentences were wordy and unclear such as the fourth sentence. The thesis statement also needed further revision because it was still vague. The body paragraph also needed further revision. After re-reading the paragraph, I realized that I needed to expound on my ideas which resulted in the formation of a subsequent draft.

****

In the following draft, I have highlighted all the corrections based on my combined revisions of Draft One and Draft Two.

Draft Three

In Ralph Ellison's "Battle Royal" and Alice Walker's "Everyday Use," each author develops his or her story on the notion that heritage is an indispensable aspect of one's life. Through the roles of the characters , the authors demonstrate that whether one chooses to embrace one's heritage in its entirety is essentially based on one's personal values, beliefs and experiences. *Furthermore*, Ellison and Walker show that each individual may choose to embrace his or her heritage at different stages in life and thus develop an appreciation for his or her culture. In "Battle Royal," the narrator–'The Invisible Man'–develops a greater appreciation for his African American heritage despite the hardships he endures during the 1930s. Likewise, in "Ev-

Comment [Teneil]: The highlighted portion is worded awkwardly and needs to be revised or deleted for clarity.

Comment [Teneil]: The punctuation surrounding this phrase needs to be revised.

eryday Use"–set in the 1970s–the character, Dee, develops a strong appreciation for her heritage. *However,* the most captivating aspect of each character's newfound appreciation is the contrast between each character's process of becoming appreciative and the distinctiveness between their resulting attitude. From an in depth analysis of both stories, one can surmise that even though 'The Invisible Man' and Dee may become more appreciative of his or her heritage, his or her understanding and appreciation of heritage will vary because of the differences between each character's path to cultural appreciation, and the influence of different perspectives on the advancement of the African American race during each character's respective time period.

Although the narrator in "Battle Royal" and the character, Dee from "Everyday Use" have both learned to embrace their heritage, there is a contrast between how each character develops an appreciation for his or her heritage. In "Battle Royal," the reader instantly becomes aware of the narrator's initial perception of shame for his culture, before experiencing the hardships of being an African American, when he overtly states: "I am not ashamed of my grandparents for having been slaves. I am only ashamed of myself for having at one time been ashamed" (Ellison 227). *However*, as the narrator describes his experience of unjust treatment and social inequality, one begins to witness his change in attitude. At the battle royal, one is able to identify the 'The Invisible Man's' initial attitude towards his race based on his perception of the other boys; he believes that he is "superior to them" (Ellison 228). His initial perception of the boys reveals

Comment [Teneil]: Punctuation needs to be revised.

Comment [Teneil]: This sentence provides more clarity to readers. The sentences are not wordy and state specific details. In addition, a time frame for each story has been established.

Comment [Teneil]: This is a hyphenated word.

Comment [Teneil]: My thesis statement is more effective. It clearly states the characters that will be discussed in the paper. The points to be addressed: "the differences between...time period," are also clearly stated thus connecting the content of the paper to the thesis statement. Despite these changes, the thesis statement could be more concise.

Comment [Teneil]: Incorrect comma usage.

Comment [Teneil]: The topic sentence needs to be more developed because it seems repetitive.

Comment [Teneil]: Who does experiencing refer to?

his misconception that his educational advancement and his submissiveness to the upper-class white men will earn him the elite white men's respect. However, though the protagonist remains oblivious to this fact by the end of the battle royal, it is evident that he is viewed as equal to the other boys because he is not exempt from the elite white men's barbaric behavior towards them. Even though there is no apparent change in his attitude towards the boys by the conclusion of the fight, the foreshadowing at the beginning of the chapter suggests that the protagonist realizes his ignorance later on in life and learns to embrace all African Americans regardless of educational status.

Evidently, the narrator has been struggling with the decision of whether **or not** he should openly embrace his roots in a society in which African Americans are viewed as inferior to the upper-class white man and have the "social responsibility" to remain submissive to their superior culture as revealed by the narrator when he exerts that African Americans should "[c]ast down [their] bucket...in making friends in every manly way of the people of all races by whom [they] are all surrounded" (Ellison 234). In fact, the notion that his fellow African Americans should become submissive to the white race is adopted from Booker T. Washington who asserted that African Americans should "exhibit good citizenship, hardwork and elevated character in order to win the respect of the "better sort" of whites" (William). Clearly, the protagonist seems to be influenced by the words of Washington. However, the protagonist's true perspective is revealed when he utters the forbidden words: "social equality" within

Comment [Teneil]: In the highlighted sentences, there is evidence of an in-depth explanation for my claim that the protagonist has a "change in attitude". In addition, I have clearly answered the questions that were asked in the previous draft pertaining to this idea.

Comment [Teneil]: This phrase needs to be deleted for clarity.

Comment [Teneil]: Sentence is too lengthy and needs to be revised.

the midst of the upper class white men (Ellison 235). His unexpected revelation not only proves that he has been affected subconsciously by the physiological and psychological abuse of the upper-class white men but it also symbolizes the beginning of his transition into an individual who accepts his background. *Undoubtedly*, the narrator's horrid experiences are gradually molding him into an individual who becomes more appreciative of his culture.

Comment [Teneil]: I have effectively incorporated research into this paragraph to support my argument. I have also explained how the protagonist's actions were influenced by an influential figure of the time period. By effectively incorporating background information, I have made my point more credible.

Comments of Draft Three

The third draft had few changes content-wise. Most of the changes are in the areas of punctuation and sentence structure. As the reader can see, there was substantial improvement in the explanation of my points, my argument was clear, and my supporting evidence from the book and research were effectively incorporated.

Below is the final draft of the revised paragraph. Based on my revision process, numerous changes and additions were made to formulate paragraphs that fully supported my argument and demonstrated innovativeness.

Final Version

In Ralph Ellison's "Battle Royal" and Alice Walker's "Everyday Use," each author develops his or her story on the notion that heritage is an indispensable aspect of one's life. Through the roles of the characters , the authors demonstrate that whether one chooses to embrace one's heritage in its entirety is essentially based on one's personal values, beliefs, and experiences. Ellison and Walker also show that each individual may choose to embrace his or her heritage at different stages in life. In "Battle Royal," the narrator, "The Invisible Man," develops a greater appreciation for his African American heritage despite the hardships he endures during the 1930s. Likewise, in “Everyday Use,” set in the 1970s, the character, Dee, develops a strong appreciation for her heritage. However, the most captivating aspect of each character’s new-found appreciation is the contrast between each character’s process of becoming appreciative and the distinctiveness between their resulting attitude. Although “The Invisible Man” and Dee become more appreciative of heritage, his or her understanding and appreciation of heritage varies because of the differences in each character’s path to cultural appreciation, and the influence of different perspectives on the advancement of African Americans during each character’s respective time period.

Although the narrator in “Battle Royal” and the character Dee from “Everyday Use” have both learned to embrace their heritage, they have varying experiences that make their individual path to cultural appreciating unique. In “Battle Royal,” the reader instantly becomes aware of the narrator’s initial perception of shame for his culture, before he experiences the hardships of being an African American, when he overtly states: “I am not ashamed of my grandparents for having been slaves. I am only ashamed of myself for having at one time been ashamed” (Ellison 227). However, as the narrator describes his experience of unjust treatment and social inequality, one begins to witness his change in attitude. At the battle royal, one is able to identify the “The Invisible Man’s” initial attitude towards his race based on his perception of the other boys; he believes that he is “superior to them” (Ellison 228). His initial perception of the boys reveals his misconception that his educational advancement and his submissiveness to the upper-class white men will earn him the elite white men’s respect. Though the protagonist remains oblivious to this fact by the end of the battle royal, it is evident that he is viewed as equal to the other boys because he is not exempt from the elite white men’s barbaric behavior towards them. Even though there is no apparent change in his attitude towards the boys by the conclusion of the fight, the foreshadowing at the beginning of the chapter suggests that the protagonist realizes his ignorance later on in life and learns to embrace all African Americans regardless of educational status.

The narrator has been struggling with the decision of whether he should openly embrace his roots in a society in which African Americans are viewed as inferior to the upper-class white man and have the “social responsibility” to remain submissive to their superior culture. The narrator reveals this notion when he insists that African Americans should "[c]ast down [their] bucket . . . in making friends in every manly way of the people of all races by whom [they] are all surrounded" (Ellison 234). In fact, the notion that his fellow African Americans should become submissive to the white race is adopted from Booker T. Washington, who asserted that African Americans should "exhibit good citizenship, hard work, and elevated character in order to win the respect of the 'better sort' of whites" (William). Clearly, the protagonist seems to be influenced by the words of Washington. However, the protagonist's true perspective is revealed when he utters the forbidden words,"social equality," within the midst of the upper class white men (Ellison 235). His unexpected revelation not only proves that he has been affected subconsciously by the physiological and psychological abuse of the upper-class white men, but also symbolizes the beginning of his transition into an individual who accepts his background. Undoubtedly, the narrator's horrid experiences are gradually molding him into an individual who becomes more appreciative of his culture.

Teneil Salmon's Peer Review Exhibit

Lending a Helping Hand

TO THE READER:

The following Peer Review Exhibit is an accurate reflection of the process I used to to review my peer's essay. Throughout the peer review process, I ensured that the author had a clear and effective thesis statement, organized her ideas in a logical manner, and employed the use of supporting evidence with sufficient explanation. I also ensured that proper grammar, clear sentence structure, and correct punctuation was used consistently throughout the paper. In general, the ideas in the author's paper needed more development and textual support, as well as appropriate research. The author had difficulty organizing her paper and presenting her ideas logically. She also needed to improve her thesis statement and topic sentences so that each paragraph related directly to her central idea. The overall content of each paragraph could also be improved by elaborating on her quotes in-depth and expounding on her ideas. I used a color scheme and commentary to clearly identify different aspects of the paper as well as to provide commendations, and suggestions for improvement.

Key For Color Code:

General Comments

Additional Explanation Needed

Grammar/Punctuation/Word Choice

Good Points

"Claims" by Judith Ortiz Cofer

Last time I saw her, Grandmother
had grown seamed as a Bedouin tent.
She had claimed the right
to sleep alone, to own
her nights, to never bear
the weight of sex again nor to accept
Its gift of comfort, for the luxury
of stretching her bones.
She'd carried eight children
three had sunk in her belly, *náufragos*
she called them, shipwrecked babies
drowned in her black waters.
Chldren are made in the night and
steal your days
for the rest of your life, amen. She said this

to each of her daughters in turn. Once she had made a pact
with man and nature and kept it. Now like the sea,
she is claiming back her territory.

()

I have yet to write the introduction because I'm not sure if I should have an introduction and then make the claim where I state that in a whole different paragraph using the research I got on Cofer, or do I just state that in my intro….I haven't decided yet. I know I stated it in my first body paragraph but I'm not sure I like that and plus there is more information I have to prove that. I'm having organization issues…it's a working progress, I need time to think. Also, I'm not entirely sure I like my thesis or if my body paragraphs actually support my thesis well enough. I need to go back and fix that. Oh and I have not written my conclusion because I'm still iffy about my thesis. I think I need to revise it more.

Thesis: In the poem "Claims", by Judith Ortiz Cofer, the speaker explains how her Grandmother is claiming her rights and her feminist views back before she became submissive and made a pact with man and nature.

In the first part of the poem, the speaker identifies the grandmother as a character who is claiming back her rights. In the first and second line, the speaker says, "Grandmother had grown seamed as a Bedouin tent" (ln 1 – 2), which interprets that the grandmother is sewing up her wounds. {Bedouins use the word} "tent" to signify a family unit that consists of a married couple, siblings, and children. This reference could mean that the Grandmother is sheltering herself, just as a tent shelters people from the outside world, from her family and claiming the right to be herself. She has sewed up the entrance to herself from the outsiders. The Grandmother may be reference to Cofer's real grandmother who she claimed to be "a homemaker and a feminist" (Cofer). If this reference is made, then the "seamed" off tent could mean that she is reasserting herself to claim back the women she was before her traditional family life.

In the next lines, the feminist ideas are enhanced by the Grandmother claiming her right "to never bear the weight of sex again" (ln 5 - 6). This frees the Grandmother from any obligation of having anymore children. This can be seen as an emphasis that the female role does not only serve as host for children going against traditional gender roles, where the female is mainly there to reproduce. Without having these constraints on the Grandmother, it gives her "the luxury of stretching her bones" (ln 7). She is able to accomplish what she wants to do, rather than what her husband or society expects of her.

While Cofer declared her grandmother as a feminist, she also claimed her to be a homemaker. The speaker contrasts the feminist ideas by explaining to the reader the eight children she bore. With eight children in the picture, one can only interpret that the grandmother had to be compliant to her gender role stereotype. Emphasizing the grandmother as the role as a homemaker, water imagery is used to explain the hardship she went through as a mother.

The speaker explains, "three had sunk in her belly, náufragos she called them, shipwrecked babies" (ln 8 - 9), these water images can be referred to as the amniotic fluid that goes along with pregnancy and the role of starting a family. Also, this water imagery can be interpreted as the storms she faced with the role of being a homemaker.

In the next section, the persona shows that the grandmother is reclaiming her old ways. The grandmother cautions her daughters and says "Children are made in the night and steal your days" (ln 13 - 14). This caution can be interpreted as the grandmother trying to pass down her feminist views to her children and try to steer them away from the traditional gender role of a housewife that she had to endure herself. This is because of the "pact" (ln 16) she made "with man and nature" (ln 17). The "pact" can be referred to as the wedding vows she said to her husband which led her to be a housewife. In addition to wedding vows and marriage, also come the traditional of life of marriage which usually includes children, and this is the "pact" that she made to Mother Nature. With the pact now complete on both sides the persona declares that the grandmother's life as a housewife is over and she is now claiming back rights as a well respected women rather than just a traditional housewife. *"Now like the sea, she is claiming back her territory" (ln 17).*

General Comments:

Overall, I think you have established your interpretation of the poem which is that the Grandmother wants to revert to her life of feminism, thus abandoning a life of motherhood. (Why do you think she wants to do this?) I think you should re-read lines three to six (ln 3-6) and lines nine through twelve (ln 9-12) for an additional interpretation. (Try to read each group of lines as one complete sentence instead of single lines.) Also, try to incorporate some more research on the author and her belief of feminism or perhaps the influence of feminism during the time in which the poem was written. In addition, you have not strayed from the general idea that was presented in your thesis. As it pertains to organization, I think that you should work on incorporating end statements and formulating more specific thesis statements. However, I believe that once you finalize your thesis statement, this will not be a major issue. I also think that your diction and tone for the essay are appropriate. Your citations from the poem are also well-done. (If you have any questions about my suggestions for your introduction, please feel free to ask).

Teneil Salmon's Wild Card Exhibit

TO THE READER:

The following Wild Card demonstrates my ability to express my personal thoughts in the form of writing. I have chosen to write an informal piece on my desire to travel because I am passionate about pursuing my goal of viewing the world. In my free write, I have utilized certain aspects of formal writing such as the correct use of grammar, variation of sentence structure and logical presentation of my ideas. My utilization of these aspects of writing illustrate that writing techniques are imperative for effective presentation of one's thoughts regardless of writing style. I have also included a few illustrations to capture the attention of my reader.

Traveling the World

Illustration 1: Central London

Illustration 2: Jamaica/The Caribbean

Illustration 3: The Opera House, Australia

Illustration 4: Venice, Italy

Illustration 5: Eiffel Tower, France

At the early age of two years old, my parents took me on my first flight from my native country to the United States for my first vacation. Although I am unable to recall the experience, I am certain that it was worthwhile. As I continued to travel throughout my lifetime, I slowly began to develop an appreciation for traveling. Needless to say, the only country I have visited is the United States of America. Despite this fact, I still have the propensity to travel to new countries so that I can become more culturally competent and also learn to embrace diversity. My desire to travel has been fueled by my acquaintance with individuals of diverse backgrounds in the United States. Within the time span of only three years, I have met individuals from Asia, Africa, the Caribbean and Europe. In some respects, I believe that I have lived my life vicariously through these individuals as I hope that I will get the opportunity to experience different cultures in the future.

The illustrations that are exhibited above show various parts of the world that I would like to explore. These countries include England, Australia, Italy, France, and the Caribbean Islands (excluding Jamaica). I believe that each country has a distinctive culture which includes scrumptious dishes, traditional dances and music, historical monuments, and a unique language or dialect. As an individual who strives to make individuals more aware of my Jamaican culture, I believe that it is my responsibility to take the initiative to learn about the culture of other countries.

My desire to travel has also impacted my educational pursuits and career goals. One of my primary goals is to partake in a Study Abroad Program in a Spanish-Speaking Country. I have chosen to travel to a Spanish-Speaking Country because I am currently pursuing a Minor in Spanish. In addition to pursuing a Minor in Spanish, I am also aspiring to become a student of International Business, which further proves that my desire to explore the world has had a strong impact on my life.

Appendix

LEARNING (YOUR FIRST JOB)

by

Robert Leamnson, Ph.D.

Introduction (*Don't skip this part*)

These pages contain some fairly blunt suggestions about what to do in college. Some of them may seem strange to you, some might seem old fashioned, and most will come across as labor intensive. But they have worked very well for many students over the past 20 years.

A fundamental idea that you will encounter over and again, is that learning is not something that just happens to you, it is something that *you do to yourself*. You cannot be "given" learning, nor can you be forced to do it. The most brilliant and inspired teacher cannot "cause" you to learn. Only you can do that. What follows are some fairly explicit "learning activities" or behaviors, but they are all your activities, and now and then those of your fellow students. But there is also a basic assumption underlying these ideas, and that's that you do want to learn something while getting a diploma. Without that desire, nothing will work.

Some words we need to understand

It happens, too often, that someone reads a passage or paragraph, as you are, and gets an idea very different from what the writer intended. This is almost always because the reader has somewhat different meanings for the words than did the writer. So that we don't have that problem here I'll make clear the meanings I intend by the words I use.

We'll start with:

Learning:

While few people think of it this way, learning is a biological process. It is indeed biological because thinking occurs when certain webs (networks) of neurons (cells) in your brain begin sending signals to other webs of neurons. You, of course, are not conscious of this process, but only of the thought that results. But there is no doubt that thinking is the result of webs of cells in your brain sending signals to other webs.

How can knowing what causes thought help in the learning process? Start by considering that human learning has two components:

1. Understanding
2. Remembering

Either of these by itself is not sufficient. Knowing a bit about how the brain works when you're thinking will help you to see why *both* understanding and remembering are necessary for learning.

Anytime you encounter a new idea (and that, after all, is why you are in college) you need to "make sense" of it, or, to understand it. And if you are actually *trying* to make sense of it, your brain is firing a lot of webs of neurons until one or more of them "sees" the logic or causality in a situation. Understanding sometimes comes in a flash and we feel, "Oh, I get it!" Other times it takes repeated exposure or the use of analogies until we finally "get it." But if we *never* get it, then we still don't understand—we haven't tried enough circuits in the brain.

So, right from the beginning, making sense of what you read or hear involves focused attention and concentration, in other words, "brain work." I'm confident that almost all college students "could" understand what is required of them by focusing attention on what is being read or heard, and stick with it until the thoughts in their heads pretty much matched those of the speaker or writer.

Unhappily, this is not the way all students in college behave. The most frequent complaint I hear from college instructors is that too many of their students are simply "passive observers." So the big rule about understanding is that it *cannot* be achieved passively. It demands an active and focused mind.

Some very bright students find little difficulty in understanding what they hear or read. But some of these smart people get very poor grades and sometimes drop out. The reason is, they neglect the second part of learning, which is *remembering*.

For most people, I suspect, remembering is more difficult than understanding. I would suggest that this is because few people know much about memory, or that it is likewise a biological process involving the firing of webs of neurons in the brain. Most people think of memories as ideas, pictures, or events that are lodged somewhere in their heads, and these places simply need to be "found." The fact, however, is that memories are not things always present somewhere in our heads. Memories must be *reconstructed* each time they are remembered. This reconstruction, in biological terms, means firing up almost the same webs of neurons that were used to perceive the original event. This would seem to be easy, *but it is not* in most cases. Here's the reason.

Use it or lose it

These webs I've been speaking of are networks of connected neurons. The details do not need to be understood, but the fact is, the *connections* between brain cells are not necessarily permanent. *Much of our brain is not hard wired.* One can think of neurons as having a big, important rule, "if the connection I made gets used a lot, it must be doing something important or useful, so I will strengthen the connection so it doesn't fall apart." And that's exactly what it does (even though, in fact, it itself doesn't *know* what it's doing.) Now the bad news. If a neuron makes a connection that does *not* get used (no matter how useful it *might have been*) it breaks the connection and it's probably gone forever. In short, neural circuits that get used become stable, those that do not get used fall apart.

So it is that we can understand something quite clearly, and some time later not be able to remember what it was we understood. The biological explanation is that the "web of understanding" was not used enough to become stable, so it fell apart.

If you've followed all of this you probably see the bad news coming. If learning means *both* understanding and remembering, we have to *practice* what we understand. Without rehearsal, that fantastic circuitry that enabled our understanding will gradually disintegrate and we can no longer reconstruct what we once understood.

Some readers are no doubt wanting to get on to the "tricks" for getting high grades. But for a lot of college courses, getting a high grade involves *only* one trick—learn the material. Learning, as described here, is the trick that always works. Learning is the goal—keep that always in mind through the rest of these pages. Grades will take care of themselves.

The Classroom

The classroom might be very traditional—a collection of students in chairs and an instructor at the front—or people seated at computer terminals, or alone at home with the computer. So long as these are in some way "interactive" with an instructor, the following suggestions will be valid and useful.

The reason something must be said about so commonplace a thing as the classroom is that too many students see it incorrectly and so they waste a highly valuable occasion for learning. The most common misconception is that the class period is that occasion when the instructor tells you what you need to know to pass the tests. Seen this way, it can only be a dreary thing, and from this perception flow a number of bad habits and behaviors that make learning more laborious and less interesting than it can be and should be.

"Taking" notes

I would like to see the expression "taking notes" removed from the vocabulary and replaced with one often used in Great Britain—that is, "making notes." "Taking" implies a passive reception of something someone else has made. It too often consists of copying what's on a chalkboard or being projected on a screen. Copying from a projected image is usually quite difficult and trying to copy what someone is saying is nearly impossible. Attempts to take notes in this way produces something that is usually quite incomplete, often garbled and has the awful effect of turning off the *listening* part of the brain. We are not capable of focusing attention on two different activities at the same time. So we miss what an instructor is saying while we concentrate on writing what he has already said, or copying from the board or screen. Some instructors compensate by making notes *for* the students and passing them out. This practice can help the better students—those who already know how to learn—but for many others it only makes matters worse. For a passive person, having a set of teacher-prepared notes means that they now have *nothing* to do during the class period. So they just sit, or daydream, or doze off, and often quit coming to class altogether. Why not, if it's all in the notes? Two more definitions will help to see that this is a recipe for failure.

Information and Knowledge

Even college professors and authors of books often confuse these words or use them interchangeably. In fact they mean very different things. Let's start with information. The world is awash in information. All the books in the library have information, as do journals, magazines, and the uncountable number of websites and postings on the internet. All of this information is transferable from one medium to another, sometimes with lightening speed. *None of it, however, is knowledge*! The reason being that knowledge can only exist in someone's head. Furthermore, the expression "transfer of knowledge" is ridiculous because it describes the impossible.

This might be a novel or surprising idea so let's examine it further. Suppose your chemistry teacher has a correct and fairly thorough knowledge of oxidation/reduction reactions. Can this knowledge be transferred to you? How wonderful if it could be. Something like a "transfusion" or "mind meld" and you know instantly what he/she knows! None of that is possible. All your teacher can give you is *information*, and perhaps the inspiration for you to do your part. This information is always in the form of symbols. These symbols might be words—spoken or written—numbers, signs, diagrams, pictures, and so on. You cannot learn anything unless you have previous knowledge of the meaning of the symbols. As a clear example, you cannot learn from someone speaking Farsi if you know only English, no matter how accurate and useful the information embedded in that language. This idea—new knowledge depends greatly on prior knowledge—will come up again later.

But if, happily, you can indeed "make sense" of new information on chemical reactions (or anything else) you can then construct your own knowledge by using the new information and incorporating it into your prior knowledge base. But, as noted above, this will involve using some not-used-before neural connections, so if you want to *remember* what you now *understand*, you must practice, that is review a number of times, or use the new knowledge repeatedly to solve problems or answer questions. Remember the rule about new knowledge—use it or lose it.

So, what do I have to do?

All of this talk about brains, information, and knowledge is not just abstract theory. It *is* the way we learn. The way to learn, then, is to align your own activities with those behaviors we already know will work.

Time

Time is nothing at all like the way we talk about it. How often do you hear someone say that they "didn't have time?" It's a perfectly meaningless expression. When you wake up on a Sunday morning, you have exactly 168 hours of time until the following Sunday morning. And everybody on the planet gets 168 hours. *No one ever has any more or any less time than anyone else!* Time cannot be "found," nor "stretched," nor "compressed," nor "lost." It cannot be "saved" or "bought," or in any other way "managed" for any realistic meaning of the word "manage." So why do we use all these meaningless expressions? It's because they let us avoid the embarrassing process of examining our priorities, a ranked list of those things we hold to be important. Sleeping is a high priority for everyone—it's a biological necessity, like food—so we all spend a fair amount of our allotted time blissfully unconscious. Now, what about the rest of our 168 hours? For someone who has to work part time to meet expenses, work is a high priority activity and they show up on schedule and on time because losing the job would mean losing the income and the consequences would be serious. So, after sleeping, eating, working, and, one hopes, going to classes, the rest of our 168 hours are spent doing whatever we find personally important. For some, doing assignments, reading books, writing reports and the like are important, so they always get done. For some others, TV, "hanging out," the internet, and partying are of primary importance, and sometimes they fill up so many of the 168 hours available that there is nothing left at the end of the week. Remember, no one gets more than 168 hours, so anyone who thinks they can "do it all" is *always* going to "run out of time."

It's your priorities and not the clock that will determine the outcome of your college experience. If it's really important, it will always get done, and always at the expense of the less important.

Studying

You and your teachers will use the word "study" frequently, and always assuming that it means the same thing to everyone. But it doesn't. For way too many college students, particularly in the first year, study never happens until just before a test. Teachers are amazed at the idea, but many students simply see no reason to study if there is no test on the horizon. So here in a nutshell is a most serious misunderstanding between college teachers and beginning students. For teachers, the purpose of study is to understand and remember the course content; for students the purpose of study is to pass the tests.

Now in an ideal world these would amount to the same thing. But in the real world, unfortunately, you can pass some tests without learning much at all. This is not the place for me to beat up on my colleagues, but some do produce truly simple-minded exams that do not require much by way of preparation. So here's an absolutely *heroic* idea if you find yourself bored with a class; try learning more than the teacher demands. Wake up your childhood curiosity and ask why other people find this discipline so interesting that they spend their lives at it. I can about guarantee that there are bright, articulate, and interesting writers in every college discipline. Find a good book and read. That way you'll learn something even if the teacher doesn't demand it.

But such "gut" courses might be rare in your college. The ones that cause trouble and hurt the grade point average are those where the teacher expects serious learning, but leaves most of it up to you. How do you cope with that?

Tough Courses

What makes a course tough? Well, sometimes it only means large amounts of material, many pages to read, lots of writing assignments, and the like. But the really tough course is one where the subject itself is complex, or presents difficult problems for the learner to deal with, and often goes faster than students would find comfortable. Suppose we add to that a super-smart teacher, but one who simply assumes you know how to learn, and sprays information like a fire hose. For a typical first year student this is the famous "worst case scenario." The whole purpose of my writing is to help you cope with worst case scenarios.

During the Lecture

In these tough courses the first idea you must abandon is that you can sit, "take" notes, and worry about it later. Here's another key idea to bring with you to every lecture period. *Worry about it* ***now***.

You can look upon your teacher as an adversary, something that stands between you and a diploma, but that's a defeatist and erroneous idea. It's better to think of the instructor as your private tutor. Most teachers welcome a considered question on the content. They nearly all resent questions like, "is this going to be on the test?" You don't do yourself any favors by giving your teachers the impression that you're a lazy goof off trying to slide by with minimal effort. Teachers can often pack a wealth of important information in what just sounds like an interesting story. They do not seem to be "giving notes." It's a serious mistake to get comfortable and daydream. When notes are not "given," then you have to make them, and that's anything but relaxing. It takes careful listening, concentration, and a focused mind to pick out the important nuggets from what appears to be a non-stop verbal ramble. A casual remark like, "there are several reasons we believe these things happen," is a clear clue that something worth knowing is coming. As noted, some teachers may pass out notes that they have made, and these might contain an outline of what's important. A fair number of college faculty have learned that this only encourages passivity and cutting classes. (It's quite easy to get the notes from someone else, and if it's only the notes that are important, why spend time sitting in a classroom?) Some teachers have discovered that students can only be prodded to serious mental activity if they *don't* provide prepared notes. This might seem mean spirited to you, but they're just trying to activate your brain.

Under conditions described above, you, to make notes from which you can learn, have to be attuned to what's being said. Not every sentence that drops from an instructor's mouth is going to contain some pearl of wisdom. Much of it is "filler" —rephrasing, giving examples, preparatory remarks for the next point and so on. You have to learn quickly where the gems are. Sentences you hear stay in the short term, immediate recall part of your brain for only a couple seconds. During that brief time you have to make the decision as to whether you've heard something important or just filler. If it was important you have to get the gist into your notes, even if that means not being quite so attentive so far as listening goes. Once it's down, refocus and wait for the next useful idea.

In short, teachers who do not "make it easy" by doing all the work, are, in fact, doing you a favor. What is often called "deep learning," the kind that demands both understanding and remembering of relationships, causes, effects and implications for new or different situations simply *cannot be made easy*. Such learning depends on students actually *restructuring* their brains and that demands effort. Such learning can, however, be most satisfying and enjoyable, even as it demands effort. I always think of serious learning of any academic subject as being something like practice for a sport or with a musical instrument. No one is born with a genetic endowment for playing either the trombone or ice hockey. These are both *developed* skills and both take long periods of concentration and effort. Both are simply difficult, but how satisfying they are as small elements are learned and burned into our brain circuits! How enjoyable to become proficient! It's exactly the same with academic matters. Give it a try.

About Interests

An obvious response to the thoughts just expressed might be, "but I like hockey, I have no interest in history," or chemistry—whatever. That may well be true, but what *is not true* is the assumption that these interests are natural — something you came into the world with. Here's another strange but important truth; *all of your interests had to be learned*! This is a small example of a paradox. You need to *know something* about a musical instrument, or a sport, or indeed, an academic subject, *before* you can judge whether or not it's interesting. But if you hold the belief that you cannot learn anything *until* or *unless* it's interesting, then you can never get started on anything new.

I was always impressed with my senior biology majors who came to my office and got around to talking about their courses in psychology, or philosophy, or art history. These students gave every discipline a chance to prove itself. Instead of depending on a teacher to "make it interesting," they studied it on their own to discover why other folk found it interesting enough to write books about it, and teach it in college. You would do yourself a great favor by developing this "curiosity habit" as early on as you can.

Between Classes

When a teacher happens not to assign some specific work to be done for the next period, a disturbing number of beginning students simply assume that means that nothing at all needs to be done. And it so happens that a lot of college instructors *do not* assign each time some reading, or writing, or problem solving to be done. And if you had an orientation session, someone probably told you that "they" expected you to spend three hours on each of your subjects, *for each hour in class*! That usually comes to an amazing 45 hours a week. Most students find that unreasonable and unnecessary, and I tend to agree. But the proper response to an excessive demand is not to do *nothing*. A huge number of new college students, when told to *study* but given nothing specific to do, simply do nothing. So here are some realistic suggestions for study outside class time.

Fill in the Notes

As noted above, it's essential during a lecture to produce some record, no matter how sketchy, of what was presented during that period. A most useful and highly recommended way to spend half an hour or so of study time is to make sense of these notes, and most importantly, turn lists and key words into real sentences that rephrase what went on. When memory fails, that's the time to use resources. Sometimes your best resource is the textbook. Even if no pages were assigned directly, there is a very high probability that the text contains, somewhere, a good, or better, description of what the teacher had presented. You may have to search for it, but tables of contents, chapter headings and the index will lead you to what you need.

Now, read with the intent of re-discovering what was presented in class. Read with understanding as the goal (this will *feel* different than reading because it was assigned.) People who know the education process thoroughly say that *most* learning in college goes on outside the classroom. So it is that you will know *more* about the day's material after this "filling in" process than when you first heard it.

But there is a further critical element here. You must *write* in your notes, in real sentences, what you have learned by the reading. Writing has an enormous power to *fix* things in the mind. *Always* write what you have learned. (Once in a while a short paragraph that summarizes or paraphrases an important aspect becomes exactly what you need on an exam. You will almost certainly remember it because you've already written it before.) There are two other good resources for filling in the notes should the textbook be insufficient. These are your classmates and the teacher (or tutor if one is available.)

Huge studies have been done to find out just what "works" for college students. What, in other words, did the truly successful students actually *do* that the unsuccessful ones did not? The first of the two most outstanding findings was that successful students had gotten "connected" to those of their teachers who were open to talking with students (and there are a lot of these.) The intent was not merely social. The point was to become more familiar with course content by simply discussing it with an expert. Remember, the successful students said that this was the *most important* thing they did to be successful. So you don't have to wonder about it; the experiment's already been done.

The second most important activity for success was to form small study groups, or pairs, with the express purpose of talking about the course content, their notes, and assigned work. Working together on assignments and problems is not cheating. Copying without learning is cheating. Discussing the details of an assignment or problem is just cooperative learning—one of the most useful habits you can develop in college. (I'm perfectly aware, by the way, that getting some guys together to discuss psychology sounds like a pretty "nerdy" thing to do. Well, so what? Really smart college students have no problem stealing a page from the "Nerd's Handbook" if it means learning more and doing better.)

Assignments

Here again, attitude will influence how you react to assigned work. To view it as paying dues, or taxes, or as mere busywork that teachers insist on out of habit, is to squander an excellent learning opportunity. Inexperienced students see assignments as something to be *done*; experienced students see them as something to be *used*. Look on every assignment as a clue from the teacher—what he or she considers important enough to spend time learning. Assignments, in most cases, are solid, meaty chunks of what's important. Don't just *do* assignments with minimal effort and thought, *use* them to learn something new.

Thoughts on verbalization

Here's another experiment that's already been done and you won't have to repeat. Things do not go into memory as a result of thinking about them vaguely—in the abstract. It has been well documented that *thought*, to be useful, must be *verbal*. Now all that means is that, to be remembered, and so useful, your thought on a topic needs to be either spoken, aloud, to another person, or written on paper. (Recall the earlier idea that information can only *move* by means of symbols, words spoken, signed, or written.) In either case, good English sentences are needed—not just word clusters. You need *verbs*. Who did what to whom? How does this thing cause that thing to happen? These facts support the suggested need to talk to teachers and classmates and *use* writing assignments to say what's true or useful. And here's a bonus! If you have filled in your notes and discussed a topic with a classmate, even if it only took 30 minutes, you will be *prepared* for the next class. That means you will have something to say should there be a "pop quiz," or if the teacher starts asking questions. Or, just as well, you can start the class by asking a well-prepared question on the last period's material. Trust me—the teacher will notice, and remember, favorably.

Access and high technology

There have been some noisy claims that today's students will turn out to be the best educated so far, *because* they have access (by way of the internet) to unimaginably more information than any previous generation. I have reservations about this claim for several reasons. For one thing, the internet has been with us for quite some time, and those of us who teach college are still looking for the promised improvement. Results should have showed up by now.

The principal reason, however, goes back to the fundamental difference between *information* and *knowledge*. Knowledge is what has the potential for improving the individual and society. But websites are completely devoid of knowledge; all they have is information (and not all of that is reliable!) No matter how many websites you have access to, none of them can do anything for *you* unless you can make sense of (and evaluate) what you find there.

And here is another little paradox I discovered by observing the differences between accomplished college seniors and most first year students. Instead of getting knowledge from the internet, *you need to have a lot of knowledge beforehand* to make sense of the ocean of information you find there.

It's tempting to believe that access to more information is going to make college easy. But it's just a temptation. You fall for it at your peril. The internet is a tool, and a very useful one, but as with all tools, you have to be knowledgeable to use it profitably.

Exams

I have intentionally put last what most new college students consider to be the single most important aspect of college—tests and exams. My reason for this approach is simple. If you attend class regularly, listen with attention, make the best notes you can, fill them in later (preferably with a study partner or two), verbalize your thoughts, and use assignments as learning tools, then you would be ready for a test at any time. Learn as you go means you're always prepared.

That is, of course, a bit overstated. In the real world, a "big test" in the offing makes even the best student nervous, and everyone bears down to some degree to get prepared. For someone who has done it all wrong, whose notes are just words copied without context or explanation, who does nothing between classes, and who never discusses coursework with anyone, and who *does* assignments thoughtlessly—just to have something to pass in—an upcoming exam is justifiably terrifying. It's these students who do everything wrong who ask embarrassing questions like, "What's this test going to cover?" or, "What chapters should we study?" They're clueless and they know it.

But let's assume you've done all the right things. You still want to do the best you can, and that means review, because stuff tends to slip out of memory, particularly when you have three or four other classes to attend to. But I mean "review" literally. It means learn again, not learn for the first time. No one can "learn" the content of 15 or 20 lectures in two days. Unless it's all completely trivial, that just can't be done. Learning a second time (real review), on the other hand, is a snap compared to learning from scratch. So, review for an exam should not be *stressful.* If you're in a state of panic because of an exam it's because you've been doing the wrong things all along.

But you're smart. You've done the right things. How do you do the review?

Don't go it alone

If you've done the right things you already have a study partner or two. Schedule firm times and places to spend an hour or so reviewing. Estimate how many days it will take to review all the material and get an early start. Don't worry about reviewing too far in advance of the exam! If you *talk* about the content and *write* summary paragraphs or descriptions, make labeled diagrams, or solve problems on paper, you won't forget—it's guaranteed. Remember, stealing a "nerd trick" will make you a better student.

Get Satan behind thee

The absolute worst thing you can do is to fall for the crazy notion that the way to prepare for an exam is to compress it all in the last 12 to 18 hours before the test, and keep it up right to the very last minute. I could always predict with great accuracy who was going to do poorly on an exam. They were red-eyed, gulping coffee to stay awake, and frantically flipping pages even as the test papers were being distributed. They had done it all wrong.

"Pulling an all-nighter," as the cute expression has it, is based on the completely erroneous belief that the only thing that college work requires is short term memory. Were that true, "last minute" study would make at least some sense. But the truth is, most college work demands thinking about, and using, a storehouse of information firmly lodged in long term memory. "All-nighter" students can usually recall a lot of terms and certain "facts," but can't do anything with them.

Remember, thinking and remembering are functions of your brain, and that's a biological organ, and significantly, it's one with limited endurance. In short, it becomes less efficient the longer you put demands on it without rest. Trying to study 12 hours without sleep has the same effect on your brain as trying to play basketball for 12 straight hours would have on the rest of your body.

So, a final rule: "Always get a night of restful sleep the night before an exam." Some students are afraid of this rule. They are afraid that sleep will somehow wipe out all they've been studying. But it doesn't! It's another of those things that have been researched and the results are consistent. There is, in fact, a small but significant *increase* in the ability to recall or reconstruct when learning is followed by sleep. So if you want your brain in tip-top condition for an exam (and who wouldn't?) do your reviewing in one or two hour periods spread out over several days, and get a real night's sleep before the exam.

During the exam

I've heard students, going into an exam, say, "I've done my part; it's out of my hands now." That idea betrays the erroneous notion that all the hard work is done in advance, and during the exam you just pour out what you've learned. Well, sometimes. But exams in the tough courses often shock beginning students because they can't find much that looks familiar. There's a reason, and a solution.

Demanding teachers prepare exams that require performance, where performance is much more than recall. A lot of college instructors produce what might be called "application questions" for their exams. All that means is that you can't just *write* what you know, you have to use what you know to answer a question or solve a problem that you haven't seen before. Only a malicious teacher would question students on material that had never been discussed, assigned, or included in required reading. It seldom happens.

So when seeing something that looks unfamiliar, convince yourself that it's only a question that is asking you to *apply* something you already know. So it is that concentration and focused thinking are often just as necessary *during* an exam as before it. If you have learned well, and reviewed properly, you can be confident that you have the necessary knowledge. It just takes some hard thinking to see how it applies to a particular question.

A Summary

No one learns unless they want to. I have assumed here that you do. But learning is a biological process that relies on the brain, a physiological organ that demands the same maintenance the rest of you does. Don't abuse it. The best ways to learn have already been discovered, there's no need for you to rediscover them by making a lot of old mistakes all over again. So it is that what you read here might be disappointing. Instead of new tricks or clever ways to beat the system, it says learning is the only way, and that learning is difficult and requires effort. But we do know how to do it, and when it's done right, it is marvelously satisfying.

I wish all readers of these pages the best of luck in their college days. But as I do so, I'm reminded of the words of the biologist Pasteur who said, "Chance favors the prepared mind."

Robert Leamnson
Dartmouth MA Dec. 2002